HOROSC
& TAROT

2024

LOVE WORK
HEALTH LUCKY

TABLE OF CONTENTS

ARIES HOROSCOPE 2024:

ARIES - Fire Sign

CHARACTERISTICS

You are characterized by your image. Stubborn as an Aries, you don't stop at anything or anyone. Bold and proud of yourself. You have an innate spirit of initiative, action, and movement. You enjoy obstacles, challenges to overcome and win. Full of yourself, you tend to dominate and subdue, sometimes even with violence. Used to being in charge, you hold prestigious positions, both in work and in interpersonal relationships. Quick and ready in your reflexes, you want everything immediately, or you let it go. You are an interesting person, but in many cases, you use and discard. In love, you experience steep climbs and steep falls. You prefer adventure to a significant love story. In love, women tend to get into trouble and complicate their lives. Danger is your profession.

ARIES GENERAL HOROSCOPE 2024

If You Insist and Resist...

... You Will Reach and Conquer

Dear Aries, welcome to 2024, a year that promises to be exciting and full of opportunities for you. But before we dive into the predictions, let's reflect on how close you have come to achieving your goals in the past year. You have been determined and worked hard, but 2024 asks you to focus on the emotions that guide your life.

Emotions and Relationships:

This year, emotions will play a central role in your life, especially in your personal relationships. The first half of the year will bring love into your life. Venus will take care of you, bringing new romantic opportunities or strengthening existing bonds. Open your heart and let love in, as it will give strength to your emotions and spirit.

Career and Opportunities:

In the second half of the year, Jupiter and Saturn will be your allies in your professional sphere. It will be a time when career opportunities abound. Keep your energy high because you will be able to achieve remarkable things in various fields. It will be the right time to embark on new projects that improve your financial situation.

Finances and Savings:

The horoscope advises you to be cautious in your expenses, at least in the first half of the year. This won't harm your reputation but will help you keep your finances under control. However, if the opportunity to travel arises, treat yourself to some relaxation. Venus suggests investing some of your savings in experiences that rejuvenate you. In 2023, Saturn influenced your intelligence and subconscious, so traveling and relaxing in the mountains might help you control your thoughts and maintain mental balance.

2024 looks like an extraordinary year for you, where emotions, love, and career will harmoniously intertwine. Keep control of your finances, but don't forget to indulge in luxury when the opportunity arises. Keep working hard and passionately pursue your goals. You are destined for great achievements and an unforgettable year. Good luck, Aries

Aries – Love Horoscope 2024

2024 promises an intense and opportunity-filled romantic experience. The influence of Venus will be a key factor in your love life, especially in the first half of the year. Here's what you can expect:

A Romantic Start

The strong presence of Venus will bring numerous romantic opportunities in the first half of the year. If you are single, you are likely to meet someone special in the second quarter of 2024. This could be the person you've been waiting for. However, remember to take the time to get to know the person better before making serious commitments.

For existing couples, this is an excellent time to strengthen your bond. Jupiter's presence in Aries makes this period favorable for considering cohabitation, marriage, or marriage proposals. Maturity will come to your relationship through the transition of the Moon in Aries' theme, but be careful not to be influenced by external interference. Keep your intimacy safe from outside interference.

Overcoming Challenges with Maturity

In the second half of the year, Mars could create negative situations to test your relationship. It's essential to avoid selfish confrontation and focus on mutual understanding. Planning a trip with your partner can help strengthen your bond.

If you already have feelings for someone, be brave in expressing your emotions. The second half of the year might be more challenging to find love, but it's not impossible. Keep searching and don't lose hope.

Marriage in 2024: An Important Step

If you are thinking about marriage, 2024 is a favorable year to do so, especially in the second half of the year. Jupiter, the planet of stability, favors Aries' marriage. However, take the time to ensure that you are ready for this significant step. Don't rush into commitments and ensure it's a well-considered decision.

Remember that your career and profession are still important, so don't sacrifice your career entirely for marriage. Maintain a balance between love and your career.

If you are divorced and want to remarry, 2024 offers you the opportunity to do so, but with caution. Take the time to fully understand the person you are about to commit to.

2024 will be a year of emotions and opportunities in love, so prepare for a romantic journey filled with ups and downs. Keep an open mind and a light heart as you immerse yourself in the adventures of love!

Aries – Finance Horoscope 2024

2024 will bring financial challenges and opportunities that require prudent management of your resources. Take inspiration from the previous year's horoscope and prepare for what awaits you in the financial sector.

Caution is Key

Saturn continues to influence your finances at the beginning of the year. Avoid overspending on luxuries and keep a vigilant eye on your expenses. This is the time to save and plan for the future. You may have the opportunity to recover money you lent to family or friends in the past, but be selective and carefully consider requests.

Jupiter's positive influence could bring benefits related to property, so consider investing in this sector. However, be cautious in your financial decisions and seek advice if needed.

Expense Management and Investments

During the third quarter, expenses may be related to your health, so ensure you have adequate coverage. Keep expenses under control to avoid financial surprises. July and August will be months with lower expenses, and you may find satisfaction in dedicating resources to your family. However, in October, be cautious with new investments, as Mars's energy could lead to hasty financial decisions. Avoid the risk of wealth loss and make thoughtful decisions. Expenses will increase again towards the end of the year, especially for leisure activities.

Regarding investments, consider the opportunity to invest in the stock market, but be wary of initial fluctuations due to Saturn's influence. Make informed decisions and seek the assistance of a financial advisor if necessary. Earnings from your business and work will remain stable throughout the year, giving you the chance to diversify your investments.

Real estate investments should be avoided in the second half of the year, as they may not be advantageous. Maintain a prudent approach to your finances and be prepared for unforeseen expenses. With careful management, you can successfully address financial challenges and seize the opportunities that 2024 has to offer. Good luck, Aries!

Aries - Career Horoscope 2024

2024 promises to be a year of growth and opportunities in your career. Prepare to reap the rewards of your dedication and successfully pursue your professional goals.

A Promising Start

2024 begins with a positive push for your business. Jupiter in the house of business will support your professional desires, but remember to avoid laziness and negative thoughts about your goals. If you are considering starting a new business, the first quarter of the year is the perfect time, as Jupiter and Saturn will bless your efforts. Sectors like real estate, food processing, metals, and wood will be particularly favorable.

Progress and Self-esteem

For professionals, the positive movement of Jupiter in your sign from May onwards will significantly improve your career prospects. Achieving your goals will be easier, boosting your self-esteem. For those seeking employment or a promotion, April will bring good news. The second half of the year will be particularly favorable for promotions, thanks to Saturn's influence on your routine work and luck. New opportunities will emerge after April.

Growing Real Estate Sector

Students preparing for competitions will need to adopt a timely schedule and put in extra effort to reach the top. Job prospects in the government seem to increase in the second half of the year, so keep making efforts to achieve your goals. In the real estate sector, Mars's support in the last three quarters will bring sudden gains and high-yield investment opportunities. However, it's essential not to rush into such investments, especially if you are inexperienced. Maintain a positive approach to work, and things will align for you.

In summary, 2024 promises growth and success in your career. Seize the opportunities that arise, maintain a positive attitude, and continue to pursue your goals with determination. Your passion and dedication will undoubtedly yield positive results!

Aries - Family Horoscope 2024

2024 brings promises of harmony and growth in your family life. Drawing from the horoscope of the previous year, prepare to build strong relationships and resolve any tensions within your family.

Family Tensions

The beginning of the year is a favorable time to address and resolve any rigidity in family life. The combined influence of Jupiter and Saturn in your fourth house will help dissolve any family issues, creating a peaceful and congenial atmosphere in your home. If there are conflicts between spouses, January, with the positivity of Venus, is a favorable time to seek a solution.

Family Growth and Harmony

In the second half of the year, prospects for expanding your family become more favorable. If you are planning to have a child, this is the best time to do so. Auspicious ceremonies may also take place in your home, bringing joy and celebration to your family.

Regarding your children, Venus's positive influence will make them more reserved. Respect their privacy, but also consider limiting their screen time. If you have an Aries child, be strict with them from the beginning of the year to prevent stubbornness from taking over. The first half of the year may present challenges, so keep an eye on your child and their company.

It is essential to dedicate time to building a stronger bond with your children. July and August are ideal months to plan family trips, creating special moments together.

By the end of the year, the solar transit will promote family growth. If you are looking to conceive, this period may bring good news. Events like marriage are favored in the second half of the year. If there have been delays in marriage matters, solutions will arrive after May 2024.

As Aries individuals are influenced by a strong Venus in 2024, it's a good year to address and resolve any pending family issues. Harmony and joy will fill your home, creating an environment where your family can thrive and grow together.

In summary, 2024 will be a year of growth and happiness in your family life. Approach challenges with love and understanding, and enjoy moments of joy with your loved ones. Your family will be your source of strength and support throughout the year. Good luck, Aries!

Aries - Health Horoscope 2024

Your health will be in the spotlight in 2024, so it's important to focus on your physical and mental well-being to face the year's challenges effectively.

Physical Activity and Well-being

Health should be one of your priorities, especially in the second quarter of the year. The strong influence of Saturn could lead to minor health issues, so it's essential to take care of yourself.

Additionally, remember that the more you focus on your health, the more you will be able to save your earnings.

To counter the effects of Saturn on your health, engage in regular light exercises and dedicate time to meditation. These practices will contribute to your physical and mental well-being.

August: Stress Management

Aries individuals, known for their hard work, may experience high levels of stress. In 2024, your mental health becomes as important as your physical health. Avoid compromising your eating habits due to work commitments. Balance your emotions to avoid unnecessary stress and anxiety.

Jupiter in the second half of the year could lead to a waste of energy. Before investing your time in new projects, make sure you have a clear understanding of your priorities and goals.

Emotional Well-being

In 2024, you may experience changes in your eating habits that could cause family tensions. Differences of opinion regarding dietary patterns may emerge. Address these situations maturely and try to manage disagreements peacefully.

If you want to lose weight, avoid refined carbohydrates and sugars, and opt for a diet rich in fruits. Consider consulting a dietitian for a personalized diet. Yoga and meditation can help you regain mental and emotional balance.

In summary, 2024 requires special attention to your physical and mental health. Practice self-care, exercise regularly, maintain a balanced diet, and take the time to manage stress. With proper care, you'll be able to face the year with vitality and well-being. Your health is the key to tackling all the challenges that 2024 has in store for you.

Couple Affinity

He Aries

Aries - Aries 91%

Aries - Taurus 78%

Aries - Gemini 62%

Aries - Cancer 57%

Aries - Leo 72%

Aries - Virgo 58%

Aries - Libra 86%

Aries - Scorpio 73%

Aries - Sagittarius 81%

Aries - Capricorn 67%

Aries - Aquarius 73%

Aries - Pisces 56%

Couple Affinity

She Aries

Aries - Aries 91%

Aries - Taurus 78%

Aries - Gemini 82%

Aries - Cancer 77%

Aries - Leo 55%

Aries - Virgo 56%

Aries - Libra 71%

Aries - Scorpio 71%

Aries - Sagittarius 76%

Aries - Capricorn 58%

Aries - Aquarius 84%

Aries - Pisces 59%

ARIES TAROT

The Aliens:

Aries seeks the Alien, they would like to have a beautiful, charming, intelligent, and preferably wealthy person by their side. Yes, everyone would like that, but they have an ideal and never settle. Because it's true that "those who settle are content," but "those who are content are even happier"!

The Fisherman:

Aries likes to court and be courted. Frankly, if the person is the right one, it doesn't take much to end up in bed, but it doesn't take long to get into trouble either. They always find people who are not available, also because by throwing out many baits, sooner or later, the tunas bite.

The Submissiveness:

When Aries is in love, meaning when they also find sexual Affinity, submissiveness is created, and the partner could make them do anything, really anything. They are even willing to financially support someone just to keep them from leaving.

The Hidden Side:

The flip side is that if Aries is not truly in love with the partner, they always end up having a "Fiesta," and we all know how parties end: the night, the alcohol, the atmosphere, and voilà, the game is over. But the next day, they would deny everything, even in the face of evidence.

Taurus – Earth Sign -

CHARACTERISTICS

You are characterized by your physicality. You have a practical spirit: among the grasshopper and the ant, you are the ant. A saver, you have a nose for business. You are stubborn, and when you set your mind on something, you don't stop until you achieve it. Prudent (not always), you are the kind one can trust. You offer and seek tranquility. You enjoy well-being, both physical, with saunas, massages, and body care, and economic. Hardworking, you think about home, family, but also material possessions. In your job, you reject roles of great responsibility, but when you're in love, you give your all. You, female Taurus, are loyal but jealous to the core. An excellent mother dedicated to the family, in life, you have only one, unique great love for whom you would do anything and more.

GENERAL HOROSCOPE 2024

"Who goes alone ... doesn't always make it big!"

Dear Taurus, 2024 opens with the need to embrace change and explore new opportunities. Looking back at the 2023 horoscope, you recognize your stubborn nature and the desire to do everything on your own, but this year is the time to step out of your comfort zone.

Facing Challenges with Patience

The first quarter of the year may present some career challenges, but do not fear. The conjunction of Saturn and Jupiter will play a significant role in shaping your destiny. Despite initial obstacles, these planets will bless you with success in love, career, and wealth later in the year.

Your patience will be tested, so practice calmness and self-control. Dedicate time to your family and strengthen your bonds with them. Venus, your ruling planet, will bring you favors both in love and in your career.

Expansion and New Connections

In the second half of the year, opportunities for expansion will open up in the business world. Have confidence in your abilities and be open to new connections. Maintain a peaceful and open attitude towards others.

In terms of love, you might feel impatient about finding your soulmate, but remember that true love can take time. This year, you will meet new people and may plan trips that allow you to make meaningful connections.

Love Pursuit and Travel Opportunities

The second half of the year could bring travel opportunities, both for personal and work-related reasons. Be open to these experiences as they can bring growth and new connections.

In the realm of love, do not aggressively seek it. Relax, meet new people, and let connections develop naturally. 2024 is a year of exploration and openings, so seize the opportunities that come your way.

In summary, 2024 challenges you to overcome your stubborn nature and embrace change with determination. Initial challenges will be overcome through your patience and planetary support. Be open to the opportunities that arise in your career and personal life. Let 2024 be a year of discovery and growth. Good luck, Taurus!

Taurus - Love Horoscope 2024

2024 will bring a wind of change and new romantic opportunities into your life. In 2023, you continued to follow your instinct to do everything on your own, but now it's time to open up to new experiences and connections.

Taking the Initiative in Love

This year, you will feel a strong need to approach someone you've known for a while. Even though it might be a challenging task for you, there's nothing wrong with taking the initiative in love. Let your intuition guide you and don't be afraid to show your interest.

For those who wish to get married, the last quarter of 2024 is the ideal time to do so. The stars favor weddings during this period, so it could be the perfect time to take this significant step.

Expansion and New Connections

In the second half of the year, Mercury and Jupiter will positively influence your marital relationship. Married couples will have the opportunity to grow and strengthen their bond. For those seeking marriage, the first two quarters of the year will bring advantageous offers.

The strong influence of Pluto in the second quarter could bring marriage proposals from afar. The Sun will also open the door to a potential spark between you and a friend you like. This could lead to mutual commitment.

Managing Conflicts and Strengthening Bonds

If you are in a dating relationship, at the beginning of the year, you may feel influenced by your partner's decisions. This could be a new but exciting experience for you. Your love life will be full of fun, and you'll have the opportunity to explore the world together.

However, be cautious not to let professional commitments negatively affect your quality time as a couple. Maintain open and honest communication to avoid misunderstandings.

The influence of Mars could bring conflicts in the relationship in the months of April and May, so make sure to stay connected during this period. If you are still single, the best time to find love is during the months of July and August, with additional opportunities in November.

Marriage and Family: A Year of Growth

The forecasts for marriage in 2024 are favorable. If marital relationships have been stagnant, 2024 could bring a solution from the beginning of the year, completely resolved by mid-March.

If marriage is on hold or if you wish to get married, the first two quarters of the year will offer favorable opportunities. The strong Venus from March to May is a favorable period to make a marriage proposal.

However, try to avoid marital conflicts caused by Uranus in the second half of the year. Mars could also cause tensions between you and your spouse, so practicing communication and behavior control will be essential. Conflicts with in-laws could emerge in August.

If you wish to have a child, plan conceptions for April, August, September, or November. As for Taurus children, encourage them to pursue a career in sports to improve their health in 2024.

In summary, 2024 will bring new opportunities and challenges in love and marriage. Be open to new experiences and wisely handle any conflicts that may arise. This year, you may find love or strengthen existing bonds.

Taurus - Career Horoscope 2024

2024 is shaping up to be a year of continued success and growth in your career. The previous year brought luck, and this trend will continue in the coming year.

Responsibility and Determination

The trio of planets, Saturn, Pluto, and Jupiter, will have a significant impact on your career in 2024. Saturn represents responsibility and determination, and its strong presence will help you develop these qualities. However, it is essential to maintain a positive mindset regarding your work and progress to reap the maximum benefit from Saturn.

The Sun, a crucial planet in your career, will connect you with influential people in your industry. These new connections could lead to new ideas and opportunities. The first two quarters of the year will be particularly favorable for promotions and job changes.

Expansion and Opportunities

Despite a somewhat slow start to the year due to the unfavorable position of the Sun, the situation will improve significantly by the end of March. From March to September, you'll have a favorable period for expanding your business or work activities. This is the ideal time to implement new strategies and tactics.

If you are involved in a family business, October will be an excellent time to sign new contracts or take on new projects. Jupiter's influence will bring significant financial gains during this period.

Finances and Investments

The final quarter of the year will focus on financial stability and investment opportunities. It's a good time to consider long-term investments or retirement planning. You may receive unexpected financial help from a family member or close friend.

However, be cautious with expenses, especially during the holiday season. Ensure you stick to your budget and avoid unnecessary indulgences.

In summary, 2024 promises to be a year of continued career growth and success for Taurus. Focus on responsibility, determination, and positive thinking in your professional life. Seize opportunities for expansion and remain mindful of your finances. With the right mindset, you can achieve your career goals and financial stability in the coming year.

Taurus - Family Horoscope 2024

In 2024, you will face challenges and opportunities in your family bonds. It will be a year in which you need to work on your understanding of family members and manage family dynamics wisely.

Family Bonds and Trends

As a Taurus native, you tend to develop a deeper understanding of family bonds when you experience them firsthand. This means you may feel distant from your family, but at the same time, you will be willing to support their needs. This tendency will be further reinforced in 2024 thanks to the positive influence of the Sun.

Keep in mind that your relationship with a sibling could become complicated, but with patience and open communication, you can overcome any difficulties.

New Milestones and Celebratory Atmosphere

The beginning of the year brings good omens for your family. A celebratory attitude and collaboration will be prominent when it comes to new family milestones. If you are considering buying a house for a move, look at the period from mid-February to March as an auspicious time for such a purchase.

Family Health Awareness

In the following months, pay particular attention to the health of your family members. Prevent them from experiencing stress and try to create a positive environment. If possible, help your parents reconnect with their old friends, providing them with companionship when you are available.

Screen Time Management for Children

Regarding your children, try to find a balance in managing their screen time. Too much time spent in front of digital devices could impact their mental health, especially mid-year due to the influence of Mars in the fourth house. Instead of imposing draconian restrictions, involve them in sports or other activities that help them develop healthy interests.

In summary, 2024 will challenge you to manage family dynamics wisely. It will be a year where you can build deeper bonds with your loved ones, overcome challenges, and celebrate family milestones. Remember that open communication and mutual understanding will be the keys to maintaining harmonious family dynamics.

Taurus - Health Horoscope 2024

2024 promises overall good health for you but will require more effort in managing your mental well-being. Here's what to expect in your health horoscope for 2024:

Continued Good Health

The good news is that your overall health will remain stable in 2024. Any past health issues will be scaled down or completely resolved. Those using medications will notice improvements from the beginning of the year.

Mental Health Awareness

However, your mental health may still be a concern. Your tendency to juggle many things simultaneously could cause stress and fatigue. This pattern persists until you reach your goals. Although your mind may face challenges, 2024 will offer creative opportunities both in your work and personal endeavors.

Mid-Year: Increased Health Awareness

In the middle of the year, you will need to be more mindful of your health. Growing responsibilities might make you feel overwhelmed, and you might neglect your well-being. This could negatively impact your family relationships. To counter this, consider adopting practices like yoga, morning walks, and detoxifying trips.

Year-End: Skin Care, Eye Care, and Diet

By the end of the year, pay special attention to caring for your skin and eyes. Reduce screen time, as it could impact your vision and skin health. If you have diabetes, be especially attentive to your condition during this period.

Take Care of Your Psyche

Finally, in 2024, make a concerted effort to work on your psyche. Focus on stress and mind management techniques. Find inner security and balance, as this will help you progress in life.

In summary, 2024 offers you good overall physical health but requires greater attention to your mental health. Find ways to manage stress and fatigue, and do not neglect your well-being as you face the challenges and opportunities that the year has in store for you.

Couple Affinity

Him Taurus

Taurus - Aries 78%

Taurus - Taurus 68%

Taurus - Gemini 61%

Taurus - Cancer 69%

Taurus - Leo 56%

Taurus - Virgo 68%

Taurus - Libra 88%

Taurus - Scorpio 80%

Taurus - Sagittarius 83%

Taurus - Capricorn 75%

Taurus - Aquarius 53%

Taurus - Pisces 82%

Couple Affinity

Her Taurus

Taurus - Aries 78%

Taurus - Taurus 68%

Taurus - Gemini 69%

Taurus - Cancer 83%

Taurus - Leo 78%

Taurus - Virgo 63%

Taurus - Libra 86%

Taurus - Scorpio 91%

Taurus - Sagittarius 81%

Taurus - Capricorn 66%

Taurus - Aquarius 90%

Taurus - Pisces 84%

TAURUS TAROT

The Minotaur:

Taurus is Taurus even in the realm of sexuality, which is why they are inclined towards beastly passions and animal instincts. This means that "something is better than nothing" is their motto. Taurus, as predictably, goes wild for lingerie, especially if it's red.

Ingenuity:

Taurus is truly ingenious; when they want something or someone, they always know how to get it. They have a way of being in the right place at the right time. Conversely, when they feel betrayed, they tend to confront the wrong person at the wrong time. They almost always find out who is betraying them.

The Faithful Servant:

Taurus's situation is somewhat reminiscent of Ambrogio and the lady with a certain longing, except that Taurus doesn't stop at just chocolates. They always know what their partner wants and can satisfy them by reading their mind. This trait is more pronounced in women.

The Hidden Side:

Taurus always knows what their partner wants, but the partner doesn't always know what Taurus wants. Therefore, Taurus often reveals a repressed Sexual Phantom, which sooner or later emerges. It's better to understand this fantasy early on before someone else does.

Gemini - Air Sign -

CHARACTERISTICS

You are characterized by communication. Eclectic, you are thirsty for knowledge. Books, poems, and sciences have been your daily bread since childhood. Confident, you are very grounded. Ambitious and changeable, if you are uncertain about something, you tend toward pessimism. Inconstant and almost never punctual, you try to achieve maximum results with minimal effort. You are attentive to your own advantage, but also generous and sensitive. You hate being alone or in the minority. You are very curious but objective in judgment. You can communicate, but above all, you can listen. You are a good friend but a difficult partner. You don't like too tight bonds, and you prioritize your head over your heart.

GENERAL HOROSCOPE 2024

Done is Better than Perfect!

Dear Gemini, 2024 is shaping up to be a year of transformations and opportunities. Here's what you can expect in your general horoscope for the year:

Focus on Transformations

After a good year, 2024 invites you to focus on transformations and changes in your life. It's the ideal time to free yourself from old baggage and aim for a more fulfilling life.

Light on the Future

Planetary transits are in your favor, paving the way for a bright future. Take advantage of this positive energy to make the changes you desire in your life.

Introspection and Personal Growth

2024 will be a year of introspection, where you'll have the opportunity to grow and develop personally. Take advantage of this period to reflect on yourself and your aspirations.

Luck and Health

Thanks to the favorable positioning of Jupiter until mid-year, you will enjoy good luck and health. This planet will support various aspects of your life, bringing prosperity and well-being.

Challenges and Success

Despite the opportunities, there will be challenges along the way, especially in the first quarter when Saturn makes its move. However, with the support of Venus and Mars, you can successfully face these challenges and pursue your goals.

Be Alert to Opportunities

Planetary transits will remind you not to overlook opportunities and to give your best to achieve success. Stay attentive and make the most of the opportunities that come your way.

In summary, 2024 will be a year of changes and personal growth for you, with the positive energy of the planets favoring your aspirations. Despite some initial challenges, the support of Venus and Mars will help you achieve great results. Prepare for a year of transformations and opportunities that will lead your life toward a brighter future.

Gemini - Love Horoscope 2024

2024 will bring a series of romantic adventures and challenges that will influence various aspects of your relationships. Here's what the love horoscope has in store for you in 2024:

Harmonious First Quarter

The beginning of 2024 will be characterized by a period of harmony in your relationships. You will free yourself from past issues and tensions, allowing you to focus on improving your romantic connections.

Pay Attention to Communication

In the first quarter, misunderstandings may arise due to the influences of Mars and Pluto. Be attentive to your communication with your partner and show how much the relationship means to you.

Opportunities in Relationships

Despite some initial challenges, 2024 offers opportunities for relationship improvement. The planet Jupiter will support the growth of deep bonds and romantic connections in the early months of the year.

Caution in New Relationships

For those seeking new connections, the planet Mercury may create obstacles. Pay attention to your words and build new relationships consciously, especially in the third quarter.

Possible Reconciliations

The last quarter of 2024 brings the possibility of reconciliations. However, the planet Pluto advises caution when welcoming people from the past back into your life. Reflect carefully before making important decisions.

Marriage and Family

Married couples will have an opportunity to strengthen their bond in 2024. However, be cautious with your words and attitudes, especially in the first quarter, as influences from the Sun and Mercury could lead to tensions with in-laws.

Reflection and New Beginnings

Jupiter will be the guiding force of your relationships in 2024, bringing optimism and new opportunities. Couples in difficulty may find new ways to look at their relationships and give them a second chance.

In general, 2024 will be a year of changes and reflections in your romantic relationships. Try to communicate openly with your partner, maintain a positive attitude, and seize the opportunities that arise. With caution and awareness, you can build stronger and more satisfying relationships throughout the year.

Gemini - Financial Horoscope 2024

2024 will bring various financial opportunities and moments of reflection. Here's what the financial horoscope predicts for your sign:

Financial Introspection

2024 will be a year of financial introspection for you. It will be important to examine your past investments and financial plans to ensure you are on the right track. Although planetary transits are generally favorable, you may encounter some obstacles along the way.

Jupiter's Blessings

Jupiter will be on your side until mid-year, bringing opportunities for long-term gains. This is a favorable period for accumulating wealth and strategic investments.

Caution in the First Months

In the first quarter, Saturn could cause some delays in your finances. Be patient and make well-considered financial decisions. Avoid financial legal issues during this period.

Success with Venus

The planet Venus will be a valuable ally for you in 2024. You will succeed in matters related to property and financial legal issues. This period is also favorable for dealing with international financial matters, such as currency exchange and international trade.

Caution with Mars

In the middle of the year, the planet Mars may bring some financial challenges. Avoid large-scale investments during this period, as they could lead to long-term losses. Instead, focus on building savings.

Lucky Last Quarter

The last quarter of the year will be promising for both Gemini men and women. You will be able to generate income from various potential sources. Venus and Mercury will support you in finding better ways to earn money from your work and investments. The planet Saturn will help attract unexpected savings from your activities and initiatives.

Long-Term Investments

If you have plans for long-term investments, 2024 might be a good time to start them, especially toward the end of the year. However, for those in the business sector, it is advisable to avoid large-scale investments throughout the year.

In summary, 2024 will be a year in which you need to take the time to carefully examine your financial situation and plan wisely. Take advantage of the opportunities offered by Jupiter and Venus, but be cautious with Mars. Focus on building savings and consider long-term investments for a more stable financial future.

Gemini - Career Horoscope 2024

2024 promises to be a year of success and growth in your career. Here's what the horoscope predicts for your sign:

Recognition and Growth

Like the previous year, in 2024, you will reach new heights in your career. You will showcase your skills and competencies prominently, earning appreciation from your superiors and colleagues. The first quarter of the year will be particularly important for your professional life.

Effort and Evaluation

Saturn will require constant effort from you, providing an opportunity to assess and improve your skills and competencies. This period will be crucial for your professional development, and you will be able to achieve significant recognition by the end of the year.

Flexibility and Collaboration

The planet Mars advises against being too rigid or finicky at work. It's important to be flexible and collaborative with your colleagues. However, don't lose your identity, and if your Mars is favorable in your natal chart, make use of your communication skills.

Promotions and Recognition

The second quarter of the year will be favorable for those seeking promotions, raises, or special recognition. The transit of Mercury will be particularly advantageous. Those working in fields related to communication, journalism, or writing will benefit from the support of Mercury and Venus.

Long-Term Growth

The planet Uranus will play a significant role in your career, bringing opportunities for long-term gains. However, avoid collaborations that could cause problems and make well-considered business decisions.

Growing Sectors

Lawyers, freelancers, and those working in sports-related professions will strengthen their foundations with the support of Saturn. Hard work throughout the year will yield results in the last quarter of 2024.

New Ventures and Work Abroad

Jupiter will be favorable for those seeking job opportunities abroad or wanting to start new ventures. This planet will instill optimism and drive you toward independence. It will also be a period of introspection to evaluate and improve your weaknesses.

In summary, 2024 will be a year of growth and opportunities in your career. Make use of the possibilities offered by planetary transits, but maintain flexibility and collaboration at work. Prepare the way for a bright professional future.

Gemini - Family Horoscope 2024

2024 will bring a series of changes and developments in your family life. Here's what the horoscope predicts for your family life in the coming year:

Strengthening Family Bonds

2024 begins with a strong focus on family bonds. You will be able to strengthen your relationships with family members in the first quarter of the year. This period will be characterized by harmony and mutual understanding.

Possible Reconciliations

For those who have faced conflicts or family tensions in the past, 2024 may bring opportunities for reconciliation. Try to resolve any differences with your loved ones and work to restore harmony within your family.

Watch Your Words

In the third quarter of the year, you will be called upon to pay particular attention to your words and tone when interacting with family members. Avoid unnecessary arguments and conflicts, especially with your loved ones. Words can have a lasting impact on family relationships.

Children and Parents

For married couples, children will play a significant role in 2024. Pluto and Uranus will have an important influence in this area. It's important to consult with a doctor before planning a family or having a child to ensure a healthy and prosperous upbringing.

Support from Jupiter

Jupiter will be a valuable ally for Gemini women looking to improve their marriage or start a family. This planet will provide positive support in these endeavors.

Avoid External Influences

Throughout the year, you may be influenced by external opinions or extended family members. Keep in mind that your family decisions should be based on your personal needs and desires, not external pressures.

Relationships with In-Laws

Newly married couples should pay attention to their relationships with in-laws, especially in the first quarter of the year. Avoid letting external opinions influence your marriage, as decisions regarding your bond should be made by you and your partner.

In summary, 2024 will be a year of strengthening family bonds and reconciliations. Pay attention to your words and actions, and strive to maintain a harmonious family environment. Be the guardian of your family decisions and follow your heart in your efforts to build stronger relationships with your loved ones.

Gemini - Health Horoscope 2024

2024 will bring a series of challenges and opportunities for your health and well-being. Here's what the horoscope predicts for your health in the coming year:

Addressing Health Issues

2024 begins with the need to address some health issues. In the first quarter, you may experience stress, anxiety, and posture-related problems, especially if you have the Gemini zodiac sign. It's important to take preventive measures such as yoga and grounding exercises to alleviate these issues.

Stress-Related Disorders

In the third quarter, you may experience minor stress-related disorders. These could include mood swings, emotional ups and downs, and a decrease in energy. Meditation and relaxation activities will be essential to keep your mind balanced and reduce pressure.

Planetary Support

With Mercury's movement in a auspicious house throughout the year, your likelihood of experiencing health issues will decrease. Mercury is your dominant planet, and its positive influence will help you overcome health-related challenges.

Challenges for Children and Seniors

Elderly individuals, children, and those who already have health problems may face additional challenges throughout the year, especially with Saturn's transit. However, over time, things will improve, and treatments and therapies will be successful.

Diet Awareness

Those with digestive issues should pay particular attention to their diet during the year. Ensure you follow an appropriate dietary plan and consult with an expert if necessary. The third quarter will make it easier to achieve your fitness goals.

Gradual Improvement

Pluto and Uranus may take you through tough times, but by the end of the year, things will stabilize, and you will achieve the desired results in terms of health and well-being.

In summary, 2024 begins with some health challenges, but with the right approach and preventive measures, you can successfully overcome them. Maintain a balanced lifestyle, pay attention to your diet, and reduce stress through relaxation practices. Ultimately, gradual improvement will lead to your healing and well-being.

COUPLE AFFINITY

Him Gemini

Gemini - Aries 82%

Gemini - Taurus 69%

Gemini - Gemini 77%

Gemini - Cancer 61%

Gemini - Leo 73%

Gemini - Virgo 82%

Gemini - Libra 68%

Gemini - Scorpio 79%

Gemini - Sagittarius 78%

Gemini - Capricorn 59%

Gemini - Aquarius 70%

Gemini - Pisces 57%

COUPLE AFFINITY

Her Gemini

Gemini - Aries 62%

Gemini - Taurus 61%

Gemini - Gemini 77%

Gemini - Cancer 78%

Gemini - Leo 65%

Gemini - Virgo 62%

Gemini - Libra 88%

Gemini - Scorpio 89%

Gemini - Sagittarius 83%

Gemini - Capricorn 69%

Gemini - Aquarius 79%

Gemini - Pisces 76%

GEMINI TAROT

The Culture:

Gemini is the cultural type; they care a lot about physical appearance, seeking a partner they can show off and introduce to their parents. They also enjoy being outside of the bedroom. But in bed, they like to explore new channels, not just the first one, and prefer a hands-on approach.

The Unknown:

Gemini loves the unknown, darkness, weightlessness, flying, and experiencing different things. Translated into a sexual context, they tend to be adventurous and may occasionally find themselves in awkward or embarrassing situations. They are known for being a bit "eccentric."

The Scientist:

Gemini always seeks new alchemies; they are not content with the same old routine. They experiment with new products, frontiers, and situations. For Gemini, sex is a bit like an erotic PlayStation. Once they start playing, they get passionate and don't stop.

The Hidden Side:

Many may dispute it, but male Geminis have a predisposition towards same-sex encounters; this can happen tomorrow, or it may never happen, but the predisposition is there, just like their tendency to form friendships. Gemini women, on the other hand, don't rule out threesomes.

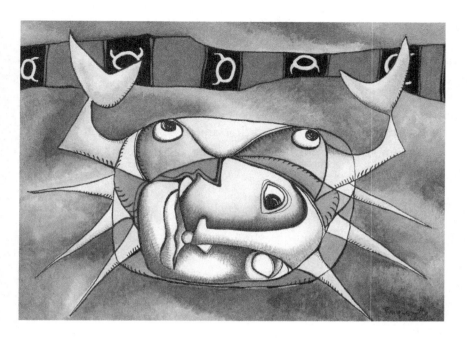

CANCER - Water Sign –

CHARACTERISTICS

Characterized by Lunacy, you are a dual sign; within you live two souls, one stable and dedicated to family, the other a lover of travel and change. You are sometimes the master, sometimes the servant. Excessive initiative contrasts with moments of sedentary life. Idealistic yet practical, cautious in your audacity. You dislike wasting and always have an extra resource when others have run out.Lively and sensitive, you can swallow toads and spit them out when they least expect it. In a couple, it's better to argue, because if you keep everything inside, in the end, you transform from Cinderella into the Wicked Witch, and it will be over forever. Faithful, the Cancer woman is one of the best mothers of the Zodiac, dedicated to home and children... but in bed, she transforms into a panther.

GENERAL HOROSCOPE 2024

A year for success!

Dear Cancer Friends, 2024 will bring a series of challenges and opportunities into your life. Here's what the horoscope predicts for your year:

Uncertain Start

2024 might begin with uncertainty and mixed results. You could feel frustrated by initial issues, but remember that you have a resilient spirit, and you shouldn't despair. Even if things seem off track, maintain your enthusiasm and determination.

Jupiter's Support

During the second quarter of the year, Jupiter will enter the Aries zodiac sign, bringing favorable situations into your life. This period will be a time when you can make significant progress and overcome obstacles. Make the most of this positive phase.

Challenges with Saturn

However, in the fourth quarter of 2024, Saturn will settle into the Aquarius sign, which could bring obstacles and delays. Nevertheless, Saturn will offer you the opportunity to reflect on your actions and decisions, helping you plan better and pursue long-term success.

Mixed Planetary Influences

Venus might be in a combust state in the third quarter, but it will still be useful to you in various ways. Pluto might make it challenging to build better social connections but will, at the same time, help you focus on personal growth. Uranus will influence your personal life and well-being, bringing a series of challenges and opportunities along the way.

Patience and Focus

Despite challenges and mixed planetary influences, you'll be guided by patience and focus throughout the year. These qualities will help you overcome difficulties and reach your goals.

In summary, 2024 might start with uncertainty, but planetary influences will change throughout the year, offering you opportunities for success. Maintain your determination and make the most of positive phases. Despite obstacles, your patience and concentration will drive you forward in your pursuit of success and personal fulfillment.

Cancer - Love Horoscope 2024

2024 will bring challenges and opportunities in the realm of love and relationships. Here's what the love horoscope predicts for your zodiac sign:

Successful Marriage Proposals

2024 starts with good news for those planning to make a special marriage proposal. Thanks to the transit of Jupiter, you'll have excellent opportunities to express your feelings and strengthen your relationship. However, you might face some challenges in long-term relationships due to Saturn's transit. Be patient and confront obstacles with confidence.

Mars Retrograde and Emotions

With the direct return of Mars early in the year, you may experience emotional highs and lows, especially if you're single. Avoid isolation and spend time with family and friends to improve your mood.

Uranus will require serious commitments, so make important decisions together with your partner.

Improved Relationships

The second half of the year will bring improvements in romantic relationships. Thanks to Jupiter and Saturn, you'll rekindle the spark in your existing relationships. Old connections may be renewed, offering new opportunities. Things will improve significantly, so don't worry about initial challenges.

Passing Tensions

The fourth quarter might bring tensions in personal relationships, especially when the Sun and Uranus act together. You might experience sudden tensions and arguments with your partner. However, these planetary influences will dissolve over time, leading to a healthier and more stable relationship towards the end of the year.

Marriages and New Relationships

Married couples will have a fantastic year, with Saturn possibly bringing up some unresolved issues but with Jupiter and Mars on your side. For those seeking to exit toxic relationships or dealing with legal matters like divorce, there will be positive outcomes towards the end of the year. Couples trying to conceive will be successful with the support of Jupiter, the Sun, and Mercury.

In summary, 2024 begins with challenges, but relationships will improve throughout the year. Be patient and confident in your pursuit of love and happiness. Married couples will enjoy a positive year, while those resolving legal issues or recovering from toxic relationships will see progress. Maintain faith in your relationships and work together with your partner to overcome challenges.

Cancer - Finance Horoscope 2024

2024 brings promises of financial success and earning opportunities. Here's what the financial horoscope predicts for your zodiac sign:

Family and Property

2024 begins with the support of your family in improving your financial situation. Matters related to ancestral property could bring gains in the second quarter of the year. However, Saturn's transit in the first quarter might lead to financial delays. Mars, on the other hand, offers opportunities to earn money, especially for those in travel-related jobs.

Business Expansion and Partnerships

Natives involved in businesses or factories will experience a year of expansion and partnerships, especially in the second half of the year. However, Mars and Saturn advise caution in making hasty investments. Be careful when dealing with others in the financial sector.

Expenses and Balance

By the third quarter, you might face some expenses, but Uranus will direct you towards savings and investments. Mercury and Mars will be favorable for your finances in the last quarter, offering opportunities to earn through travel and work.

Investment Tips

Despite planetary support, avoid making impulsive investments. Consult industry experts and make informed decisions. Mars and Saturn will keep you on alert throughout the year, so pay close attention. For short-term investments or in the stock market, the period towards the end of 2024 will be more favorable.

In summary, 2024 promises wealth accumulation and financial opportunities. Be cautious in financial decisions and seek advice when necessary. Businesses related to travel and commercial partnerships will see significant growth. Maintain a balanced financial mindset and make the most of earning opportunities in the last quarter.

Cancer - Career Horoscope 2024

The Cancer career outlook for 2024 predicts a series of opportunities and challenges. Here's what you can expect for your zodiac sign in terms of career during the year:

Professional Opportunities:

2024 may bring many career opportunities for you, especially in the first two quarters of the year. You'll be able to showcase your skills and gain the recognition you deserve. This is a good time to seek career advancements, change jobs, or take on new professional challenges.

Creativity and Innovation:

It will be a year where you can display your creativity and innovative thinking. Your original ideas will be appreciated by your superiors and colleagues, leading to exciting projects and increased involvement in your profession.

Interpersonal Relationships:

Effective communication and interpersonal relationships will be crucial for success in your career in 2024. Building positive relationships with colleagues, superiors, and clients will be key to your professional progress. Your ability to work in teams and manage interpersonal dynamics will be a critical factor in your career advancement.

Balancing Work and Personal Life:

Despite career opportunities, it's essential to balance work with your personal life. Ensure you dedicate time to your family and personal interests to avoid burnout. A balanced life will contribute to your overall happiness and professional success.

Financial Planning:

Pay attention to financial planning throughout the year. Even though earning opportunities are present, it's essential to manage your finances wisely. Create a long-term financial plan and save for the future.

Continuous Learning:

Consider investing in your ongoing education. Learning new skills and additional training could be beneficial for your long-term career.

2024 offers numerous career opportunities for Cancer individuals, but it will also require commitment, effective communication, and a good balance between work and personal life. Be open to challenges and opportunities that come your way, and you'll be able to make significant career progress.

Cancer - Family Horoscope 2024

2024 promises a range of family experiences, with ups and downs. Here's what the family horoscope predicts for your zodiac sign:

Family Support and Shared Success:

In 2024, family support will be a significant pillar for your well-being. Family members will be a source of mutual support, contributing to the professional and financial success of all. Some may receive good news from siblings and close individuals. This climate of support and success will be a positive aspect of your year.

Emotional Challenges:

However, Pluto and Uranus may bring mood swings and heated discussions within the family. These planets could cause emotional turmoil and obstacles in family relationships. Patience and understanding will be key to overcoming these difficult moments.

Jupiter: Confidence and Communication:

Jupiter will be a valuable ally, providing self-confidence and improving your communication within family dynamics. You might address issues from the past, some of which could lead to tensions, especially regarding significant decisions like marriage. It will be important to stay calm and seek peaceful resolutions with your family.

Family Health:

In 2024, the health of family members will generally be good. However, you might experience some health issues with your mother around the second quarter. Ensure she takes care of herself and avoids stress and strain. Pay attention to road safety, as there could be risks of accidents and injuries to family members.

Relationships with In-Laws:

Married Cancers might have to deal with challenges related to in-laws. Some may feel distant from the family due to disputes or tensions. It's essential to remain calm, communicate openly, and work to resolve issues peacefully, avoiding damaging arguments within the family environment.

In summary, 2024 will bring a mix of family support and emotional challenges. Make the most of family support for professional and financial success, but remember to address family issues with patience and open communication.

Cancer - Health Horoscope 2024

2024 will be a year when you'll need to pay special attention to your health and well-being. Here's what the health horoscope predicts:

Saturn's Influence:

Saturn will continue to influence your health throughout the year. You may experience moments when things seem under control, but you'll also feel some restlessness and fatigue. These signals are a warning not to neglect your health. Saturn reminds you that carelessness could lead to unexpected complications.

Staying Calm:

Don't let the stresses of daily life affect your mood. Saturn might bring stressful situations, but it's crucial to stay calm and face them with patience. Don't take your health lightly and look for signs that might indicate issues.

Jupiter: Positive Changes:

In the second half of the year, with Jupiter's return, you may experience improvements in your health. Therapies, medications, and treatments that seemed ineffective will start working in your favor. Maintain optimism about your health and don't prematurely abandon treatments.

Relaxation and Vacations:

Mental health is just as important as physical health. Mercury and the Sun may bring moments of stress, but try to accept challenges in the best way possible and take time to relax. A break, a vacation, or a trip with your family can help revitalize your mind and renew your energy.

Fitness and Nutrition:

If you're passionate about fitness, it's essential not to overdo it. Pluto and Uranus might negatively affect your health and well-being. Practice meditation, yoga, and chakra balancing to relax and reduce stress. Pluto might tempt you with unhealthy eating habits, so focus on maintaining a healthy diet.

In summary, 2024 will require you to manage your health wisely. Pay attention to the signals your body sends and don't neglect your physical and mental well-being. Stay calm in the face of stress and changes, and don't hesitate to seek medical support when needed. Your health is your most precious wealth, so take care of it with care.

Couple Affinity

Him, Cancer

Cancer - Aries 77%

Cancer - Taurus 83%

Cancer - Gemini 78%

Cancer - Cancer 63%

Cancer - Leo 68%

Cancer - Virgo 61%

Cancer - Libra 69%

Cancer - Scorpio 79%

Cancer - Sagittarius 84%

Cancer - Capricorn 73%

Cancer - Aquarius 58%

Cancer - Pisces 89%

Couple Affinity

Her, Cancer

Cancer - Aries 57%

Cancer - Taurus 69%

Cancer - Gemini 61%

Cancer - Cancer 63%

Cancer - Leo 63%

Cancer - Virgo 76%

Cancer - Libra 73%

Cancer - Scorpio 78%

Cancer - Sagittarius 79%

Cancer - Capricorn 71%

Cancer - Aquarius 68%

Cancer - Pisces 71%

CANCER TAROT

Dual Personality:

Cancer has a dual personality. Especially the woman, as kind and sweet as she is in affection, she can be aggressive in intimacy. Sometimes she likes to take the initiative, and other times she wants her partner to take it. With Cancer, never take anything for granted.

The Explorer:

Cancer likes to explore new horizons, but being Cancer, they tend to approach situations sideways rather than head-on. They have a strong shell and are the Indiana Jones of sex. They rarely indulge in public displays of affection, but in private, they have hidden talents that only those who have experienced them know.

The Slave:

As we've seen, Cancer is dual, so sometimes they are the slave, but at other times, they are the master. They like to feel like Cinderella, always searching for Prince Charming, but they seek more than just looks. Yes, they can be a slave, but it's all for love.

The Hidden Fear:

Cancer's fear is Impotence, not the kind cured by Viagra, but the inability to do something. They tend to partner with someone who is in high demand on the market, but then they have to fight tooth and nail to hold onto them. Just the thought of losing them drives them crazy.

LEO - Fire Sign –

Characteristics

You are characterized by excess. You have a strong sense of pride and dominance, especially in the workplace. Sometimes, you can become despotic and treat colleagues and subordinates in a less delicate manner. You are very independent but do not compromise on your morals. Fundamentally good and likable, but very, very proud. You like money not out of greed but as a means to buy what you desire – and Leo likes to shop! For you, success is not a hypothesis but a certainty. Your impulsiveness can sometimes lead to violence, especially in romantic relationships. You are generous and live your loves with passion and frankness. You only feel jealous if there is a valid reason.

General Horoscope for 2024

Who starts well... is halfway through! 2024 has finally arrived and shines like a ray of sunshine in your life. This year will be a mix of challenges and opportunities, but in the end, you will come out stronger and happier. Here's what awaits you in the Leo horoscope for 2024:

Chaotic Beginnings, but a Bright Ending

2024 starts with some challenges and confusion due to the influence of Saturn. However, remember that every beginning can be a bit chaotic. Stay calm and accept that you deserve a break to reflect and relax. Be open to new experiences and adventures that may take you in unexpected directions.

Bright Love and Relationships

The energy of Venus will shine in your love life for most of 2024. You will be inspired to express your feelings and experience extraordinary romantic moments. Keep an eye on March when romantic interactions will be particularly favorable. Put aside shyness and follow your heart.

Career and Work

Your career might be at the center of your concerns in the middle of the year. Work-related issues may arise, but it's essential to maintain a positive attitude. Work on practical solutions and seize opportunities to improve your professional position.

Health and Well-being

Your health will require attention throughout 2024. Saturn could cause moments of fatigue and confusion. Take time to rest and take care of yourself. Don't ignore your body's signals, and try to adopt a healthier lifestyle.

Joy and Success

Towards the end of the year, the positive influence of Jupiter will begin to manifest. It will be a time when everything seems to fall into place. Enjoy the opportunities that come your way and rejoice in the successes you will achieve. 2024 will offer you many reasons to be happy.

In summary, 2024 will be a year of personal growth and success for Leos. Face the challenges with determination and embrace the opportunities that come your way. With love, dedication, and a positive attitude, you will reach new heights of joy and success.

Leo - Love Horoscope 2024

2024 will be a year of ups and downs in love and relationships. It will be a period in which you can experience many emotions and challenges. Here's what to expect for your love life in 2024:

Start with Challenges to Overcome

2024 will begin with some love challenges due to the influence of Saturn. You may face controversies and conflicts, both in existing relationships and in your search for new love. It's essential to avoid bringing up the past and work to resolve differences maturely.

Favorable for New Relationships

If you are single and looking for love, 2024 will offer opportunities to start new relationships. However, avoid seeking quick answers and be patient in approaching new people. The third quarter of the year will be particularly favorable for forming new romantic bonds.

Strengthening Marital Relationships

Married couples will have the opportunity to strengthen their bonds in 2024. Use the energy of Venus in the middle of the year to enhance your relationships with in-laws and spend quality time with your partner. The second half of the year will be ideal for those who wish to further commit or get married.

Facing Challenges with Maturity

2024 may bring some relationship challenges, but it's essential to address them maturely. Ego may cause issues, but working together to solve problems will be crucial. Plan activities that allow you to experience new things with your partner.

Marriages and Divorces

If you are thinking of getting married, consider the second half of the year to do so, especially if you want the blessings of a strong Jupiter. On the other hand, those going through a lengthy divorce process may finally achieve the desired freedom by the second quarter of 2024.

Avoiding Temptations

Temptations outside of marriage may arise, but it's crucial to resist them. Maintain open communication with your partner to avoid stressful situations in the relationship. Remember that the challenges will be temporary and solvable through communication.

In summary, 2024 will bring highs and lows in love and relationships for Leos. Face the challenges with maturity and work to resolve issues with your partner. It will also be a year where you'll have the opportunity to start new relationships or strengthen existing bonds. Be patient, open, and ready to experience new romantic adventures.

Leo - Finance Horoscope 2024

2024 will bring a series of significant financial considerations into your life. It will be a year where you need to be wise in your financial decisions and plan carefully. Here's what to expect in your finances in 2024:

Avoid Dwelling on the Past

At the beginning of the year, a powerful Saturn reminds you of the importance of avoiding dwelling on the past. Instead, focus on actions that will help you build a solid financial future. In the first quarter, significant financial changes are not expected, and negative Mars could delay success. Stay calm and don't let frustration push you toward impulsive decisions.

Explore Investment Opportunities

In the second quarter, you'll feel inspired to explore investment opportunities. Make informed financial decisions during this period, as your investments may bring profits in the second half of the year. Saturn will continue to influence your finances, so you may experience delays in business income.

However, if you work for a company, there are good chances of raises and promotions, along with opportunities for business travel.

Leo women should be particularly mindful of expenses during this period. Establish a budget and try to stick to it.

Benefits from Jupiter in the Third Quarter

The third quarter of 2024 will see a strengthened Jupiter in the Leo horoscope. You will have a higher chance of recovering borrowed money during this period. Jupiter will also support family businesses, especially those related to home furnishings. Additionally, there will be earning opportunities from property and agriculture investments. October 2024 is a good time to purchase a vehicle. Make sure to make informed decisions, as Jupiter represents knowledge.

Spend Wisely in the Last Quarter

In the final quarter, you will need to deal with expenses, especially related to leisure activities, that you won't regret. Hoarding money won't be helpful as there will be many reasons, especially related to children, that will require expenses. Don't hold back your desires in an attempt to save money. Instead, leisure or shopping expenses in December 2024 will strengthen Venus's position in your Ascendant. This will bring more romance and good luck into your life.

In summary, 2024 requires wisdom in financial decisions. Plan carefully, make informed investments, and don't let frustration or impulsivity influence your financial choices. With prudent management of your finances, you can approach the year with confidence and financial stability.

Leo - Career Horoscope 2024

2024 will bring a series of challenges and opportunities in your career. It will be a year where you'll need to put in your commitment and determination to achieve your goals. Here's what to expect in your career in 2024:

Supported by a Strong Jupiter

A strong Jupiter will be on your side in 2024, ready to support your professional efforts. This planet will bring positive energy that will help you grow in your career. However, you'll need to put your commitment into action from the beginning of the year.

Challenges for Students

Students seeking career opportunities through government exams may face some challenges. Pluto and Saturn could bring delays and distractions in the first quarter. Extraordinary commitment will be required to overcome these challenges.

Job Opportunities Abroad

Those seeking job opportunities abroad will have better prospects in the second quarter of 2024. This could be the ideal time to explore international opportunities and make progress in your career.

Health and Career

At the beginning of the year, health-related issues may affect your career or studies. It's essential to take care of your health without feeling guilty about the need for rest. Patience and perseverance will be crucial in achieving your professional goals.

Business Growth

Businessmen will see an increase in sales in the first quarter of 2024. Growth and expansion in business will be particularly favorable in the third quarter, with Jupiter inspiring you with innovative ideas.

Self-Realization and Motivation

The third quarter will be a time of self-realization. It's the best time for students preparing for government exams, thanks to the motivation provided by Jupiter. Professionals may feel demotivated, but it's a time to reflect on their future strategies.

Fruits of Business Expansion

In the last quarter of 2024, professionals will reap the rewards of business expansion. It's a good time to pursue professional courses related to your career or business activities. Training and growth opportunities will be available.

In summary, 2024 will be a year where you need to put your commitment and determination into achieving success in your career. Be prepared to face challenges, but also take advantage of the opportunities that come your way. Use the positive energy of Jupiter to your advantage and work diligently to achieve your professional goals.

Leo - Family Horoscope 2024

2024 seems to bring some challenges in relationships but also opportunities to improve your relationship with loved ones. Here's what you can expect for your family and relationship health throughout the year, taking into account astrological influences:

Caution in Marital Relationships

2024 seems to bring some challenges in marriages. The horoscope suggests being cautious in dealing with your spouse and avoiding immature behavior or offensive words. Communication and mutual respect will be crucial in overcoming these obstacles. However, there's good news: your relationship with your in-laws will improve, bringing a sense of harmony to your family.

Blossoming Romantic Relationships

Thanks to the transit of the Sun in the horoscope, romantic relationships, both among married and unmarried couples, will bloom in 2024. This will bring a new level of connection and affection between you and your partner. It's a good time to strengthen your bond.

Spiritual Tours and Child Care

From January to April, it's a favorable period for spiritual tours, especially if you have children. However, if you're a parent of teenagers, it's essential to monitor their screen time and try to reduce it. Make sure they are not distracted from things that matter for their overall growth. Spend quality time with your children and try to avoid conflicts or arguments when you're with them.

Children to Come and Celebrations

For couples desiring to have a child, February and August are the best months to try to conceive. If you're already pregnant, take care of yourself by avoiding excessive screen time and investing time in arts and crafts to enhance your child's intellect. Additionally, toward the end of the year, there are good chances for celebrating an auspicious ceremony at your home.

In summary, 2024 will bring some relationship challenges but also the opportunity to strengthen family bonds. It's essential to stay calm, communicate openly, and seek moments of connection with your loved ones. Also, pay attention to family details and take care of your mental health.

Leo - Health Horoscope 2024

2024 appears to bring a good dose of well-being for your health. Here's what you can expect for your health throughout the year:

A Good Start with Some Warnings

The first quarter may start with some health-related challenges due to the presence of Saturn and Pluto. However, these challenges will be successfully overcome, and starting from the second quarter, you'll see a significant improvement in your health. It's important not to become lazy or neglect your efforts to maintain good health even when things seem to be going well.

Eye Care

One cautionary note pertains to eye health. The horoscope suggests that you may experience eye fatigue during the year, possibly due to prolonged use of digital devices. Make sure to take care of your eyes by eating healthily, regularly washing them, and, if necessary, wearing computer glasses.

The Importance of Physical Exercise

Maintaining a regular exercise regimen will be essential for your health. Running and consistent workouts will help you stay in shape and manage stress. Physical activity is an excellent way to improve your mental and physical well-being.

Mental Health Matters

2024 may bring challenges in terms of mental health due to issues related to marriage, career, or personal growth. It's crucial to maintain a positive outlook on life and practice techniques like yoga and meditation to stay calm and clear-headed. Short naps during the day can also help refresh your mind.

Prevention for the Elderly and Younger Leo

For elderly and older Leos, there are no significant health issues on the horizon, but it's important to follow preventive measures and maintain a balanced diet. For younger Leos, especially those who enjoy outdoor activities, it's essential to be cautious to avoid injuries due to carelessness.

In general, 2024 appears to be a year of good health for you, but it's crucial to continue taking care of yourself and follow a self-care routine to make the most of this positive energy throughout the year.

Couple Affinity

Him Leo

Leo - Aries 72%

Leo - Taurus 78%

Leo - Gemini 78%

Leo - Cancer 63%

Leo - Leo 55%

Leo - Virgo 78%

Leo - Libra 92%

Leo - Scorpio 56%

Leo - Sagittarius 75%

Leo - Capricorn 80%

Leo - Aquarius 81%

Leo - Pisces 58%

Couple Affinity

Her Leo

Leo - Aries 89%

Leo - Taurus 56%

Leo - Gemini 65%

Leo - Cancer 68%

Leo - Leo 55%

Leo - Virgo 51%

Leo - Libra 89%

Leo - Scorpio 78%

Leo - Sagittarius 83%

Leo - Capricorn 69%

Leo - Aquarius 77%

Leo - Pisces 75%

Leo Tarot

The Goddess:

Leo, especially Leo women, likes to be constantly admired and adored. She enjoys being showered with compliments and hearing that she is the most beautiful, talented, and unique person. If you fail to do so, she may distance herself.

The Voyeur:

Leo has a bit of an exhibitionist streak and enjoys being noticed. They can stimulate their partner's imagination even while doing everyday activities like walking, doing the dishes, shopping, or simply smoking a cigarette. This sometimes leads them to have relationships outside the bedroom.

The Aristocrat:

When it comes to sex, Leo is very refined. There are more sophisticated pleasures that Leo is aware of, and they are either known or not known. If a partner practices them without Leo uttering a word, the relationship will continue; otherwise, it may not have a great future.

The Hidden Side:

Despite being the king of the jungle, Leo remains an incurable romantic. Dates and special occasions are not just important but crucial to Leo. Surprises and unexpected gifts are also very much appreciated, and Leo knows how to reciprocate in kind.

VIRGO - Earth Sign –

Characteristics

You are characterized by precision. Practical and cautious, you are a cool-headed individual. Gifted in studying, you love plants and animals. Calm and collected, you are the anchor for restless people. You are also meticulous at work, analyzing situations from all angles. Intelligent, you can be the right person at the right time. Organized and clean, you border on being intolerant. Despite being lucky, you always remain realistic, favoring the soul over the body. You are sweet and understanding with everyone, but you don't let anyone walk all over you. Deeply jealous in romantic relationships, you, as a Virgo mother, tend to be overly apprehensive. If you don't find your soulmate, you are inclined to remain single; not like the Findus frozen food, for whom all seasons are good for picking peas.

2024 General Horoscope

A year full of possibilities

2024 brings a new set of challenges and opportunities, and your natural wisdom will guide you through this year. Here's what you can expect for 2024, considering the astrological influences:

Reconsidering the Past

Your reflective nature often leads you to reexamine the past, but this year, the horoscope advises you to avoid getting stuck in regrets over missed opportunities. Instead, focus on practical answers to the questions that plague you at the beginning of the year, so you won't miss further opportunities in 2024.

Professional Success and Love Relationships

The strong presence of Jupiter in the Virgo 2024 horoscope promises good opportunities for professional success, marriage, and even conceiving a child starting from the second quarter. Venus's influences throughout the year will favor love relationships, bringing greater affection and connection between you and your partner.

Travel and Financial Opportunities

Thanks to Mars and Mercury in your natal chart, you'll have many travel opportunities from the beginning of the year. Some of you may even earn money through travel or related activities. However, towards the end of the year, Uranus' transit suggests paying attention to relationships and financial matters.

Professional Opportunities in Research or Legal Fields

Professional opportunities will be abundant in 2024, especially if you work in research or the legal field. Keep in mind that Uranus and Mars could influence the legal sector in the third quarter, so be honest and professional in your work. Additionally, in business activities, try to avoid conflicts with colleagues. A strong Venus will give you the opportunity to form romantic bonds with a colleague.

Patience and Reevaluation

The Virgo 2024 horoscope advises you to be patient and carefully reflect on your actions. While your determination and commitment are virtues, this year might be a time to consider alternatives and evaluate if there are different ways to achieve your goals.

In summary, 2024 offers significant opportunities both professionally and personally. Your ability to reflect and your wisdom will guide you through this year. Be open to new possibilities and make the most of the opportunities that come your way.

Virgo - Love Horoscope 2024

2024 will be a year where you will navigate the waters of relationships and emotions. Here's what the love horoscope predicts for your sign, considering what happened in 2023:

Rediscovery of Past Relationships

2024 might bring a rediscovery of past relationships, with the blessing of Jupiter in your astrological chart. Past issues might find resolutions, and the lost spark in marriages could be reignited. Be romantic and expressive with your partner, as this will strengthen your bond as a couple.

Resolving Couple Issues

In the first quarter of the year, some conflicts might emerge in your relationship. Keep in mind that dwelling on past mistakes might worsen things. Avoid unnecessary arguments, especially if they aim to hurt your partner's ego.

Regarding Family and Marriage

Thanks to the transits of Jupiter and Pluto in the second quarter, you will be encouraged to be cautious about secret love affairs or morally questionable bonds. If you plan to propose or ask someone to marry you, June is the best time to do so, but do it gracefully and elegantly. July and August are ideal months for love weddings.

Patience and Reconciliation

The second half of the year will bring resolutions for those seeking divorce or involved in legal battles related to marriage. Avoid conflicts with in-laws, maintain maturity, and consider the possibility of reconciliation, as Jupiter becomes stronger in your love life.

In summary, 2024 will be a year of ups and downs in love relationships for Virgo. It will be a period of reconciliation, rediscovery, and for some, new romantic beginnings. Maintain maturity and patience in every situation, and it will help you overcome challenges and enjoy moments of love and happiness the year has to offer.

Virgo - Finance Horoscope 2024

2024 brings a series of astrological influences that will impact your personal finances. Here's what you can expect in terms of finances for your zodiac sign during the year:

The year 2024 starts with some financial challenges. Expenses may rise while sources of income could be limited. It's crucial to avoid hasty financial decisions during this period. Planetary conjunctions might lead to losses if you don't act with caution.

In the second quarter, your finances might slightly improve. If you're considering changing jobs, this could be a good time to do so, as you might receive a salary increase or a new professional opportunity that contributes to your earnings.

The middle of the year could bring greater financial stability. Earning opportunities may come through new projects or collaborations. If you've been saving for an overseas trip, this might be a good time to make it a reality.

Towards the end of the year, your income might further increase. You could receive a raise or an additional source of earnings. However, the horoscope warns you to avoid excessive spending and to plan your finances carefully.

Financial Advice:

Careful Management: Be mindful of your expenses and try to save when possible. Avoid hasty financial decisions.

Prudent Investments: If you're considering significant investments, such as property, make sure to do so after the second quarter of the year when astrological influences are more favorable.

Long-Term Planning: Create a long-term financial plan and save for the future. Take care of your finances responsibly.

Avoid Unnecessary Expenses: Steer clear of unnecessary expenses and think carefully before making costly purchases.

Financial Education: If you haven't already, invest in financial education. Learn how to manage your money efficiently and invest wisely.

Balance Between Saving and Enjoyment: Find a balance between saving for the future and enjoying life in the present.

2024 might bring financial ups and downs for Virgo. It's essential to manage your finances carefully, plan for the future, and make wise financial choices. With proper planning, you'll be able to navigate challenges and seize the opportunities that come your way throughout the year.

Virgo - Career Horoscope 2024

2024 promises significant changes and opportunities in your professional life. This year will be a time of growth and achievement for you, provided you're willing to take risks and adapt to the new scenarios that unfold. Here's what awaits you in your career for 2024:

New Opportunities:

The year 2024 may begin with the arrival of fresh career opportunities. Be ready to seize them, even if they involve a change in your routine or pose a challenge. These opportunities will help you grow and advance in your career.

Innovation and Creativity:

Virgo is known for precision and attention to detail, but this year, you should also embrace your creativity. Innovation will be a key to success in 2024, so look for new and original ways to tackle professional challenges.

Skill Development:

This is the ideal time to invest in your professional growth. Consider acquiring new skills or deepening existing ones. This will make you more competitive in the job market and open up new doors for you.

Professional Relationships:

Relationships with colleagues, superiors, and collaborators will be crucial this year. Be open to collaboration and effective communication. The alliances you form now could lead to future opportunities.

Focus on Health:

To support your professional success, it's essential to take care of your physical and mental health. 2024 requires a good balance between work and personal life, so make sure to find time for rest and well-being.

Clear Goals:

Set clear and realistic career goals for 2024. This will help you stay motivated and measure your progress. Work diligently towards these goals and don't be discouraged by temporary setbacks.

Remember that 2024 will be a year of growth and achievement, but it will require commitment and flexibility from you. Approach challenges with confidence, and you'll be able to reach your professional goals.

Virgo - Family Horoscope 2024

2024 will bring significant developments in your family and personal relationships. It will be a year where you can strengthen existing bonds and create new meaningful connections. Here's what you can expect in your family and personal relationships for 2024:

Strengthening Family Bonds:

This year, dedicate more time to your family. It will be a favorable period for strengthening existing family ties and resolving any past conflicts. Your dedication to the family will be rewarded with love and unconditional support.

New Friendships and Connections:

Be open to meeting new people. In 2024, you might make new friendships that prove valuable in your life. These connections could come from different environments, so be prepared to expand your social circle.

Mutual Understanding:

Make an effort to understand others' perspectives. In 2024, situations may arise that require empathy and tolerance. Show understanding toward others' challenges and viewpoints to maintain harmonious relationships.

Balance:

Find a balance between the time you dedicate to family and personal relationships and your professional commitments. Balancing these aspects of your life will be crucial for your overall well-being.

2024 offers the opportunity to create stronger and more meaningful bonds in your family and personal relationships. With openness, effective communication, and dedication, you can navigate challenges and enjoy the rewards this year has to offer

Virgo - Health Horoscope 2024

In 2024, it's important to emphasize that your health will be influenced by managing anger, attention to detail, and connecting with nature. Here are some tips for maintaining good health throughout the year:

Managing Anger:

Controlling anger will be crucial for your well-being. Find healthy ways to express it through physical exercise.

Balanced Diet:

Eating a balanced and nutritious diet is essential for your physical and emotional health. Include fruits, vegetables, lean proteins, and whole grains in your diet.

Relaxation and Self-Reflection:

Allocate time for relaxation and self-reflection. Moments of tranquility will help you manage stress and maintain emotional balance.

Open Communication:

Communicate openly with your partner or spouse to reduce conflicts and improve emotional well-being.

Family Health:

Pay attention to the health of your children and elderly family members until June 2024. Don't neglect routine medical check-ups and provide support when needed.

Natural Remedies:

Explore natural remedies and reduce reliance on medications. Avoid excessive use of sleep aids or painkillers and look into natural alternatives.

Nature Connection:

Indulge in spending time in nature. Visiting waterfalls or natural settings during a trip can contribute to your overall well-being.

Skin Health:

Be attentive to skin issues, especially in the last two quarters of the year.

Pregnancy:

If you are expecting, the third quarter might be the best time for pregnancy. Reduce stress, limit screen time, and explore methods to improve mental health for both you and your child.

2024 appears to promise good health for Virgo individuals. Just remember to take care of yourself, manage stress effectively, and listen to your body. With proper attention, you can enjoy a year of health and well-being.

Couple Affinity

Virgo Man:

Virgo - Aries 56%

Virgo - Taurus 63%

Virgo - Gemini 62%

Virgo - Cancer 76%

Virgo - Leo 51%

Virgo - Virgo 82%

Virgo - Libra 69%

Virgo - Scorpio 76%

Virgo - Sagittarius 63%

Virgo - Capricorn 71%

Virgo - Aquarius 78%

Virgo - Pisces 69%

Couple Affinity

Virgo Woman:

Virgo - Aries 58%

Virgo - Taurus 68%

Virgo - Gemini 82%

Virgo - Cancer 61%

Virgo - Leo 78%

Virgo - Virgo 82%

Virgo - Libra 69%

Virgo - Scorpio 73%

Virgo - Sagittarius 59%

Virgo - Capricorn 78%

Virgo - Aquarius 76%

Virgo - Pisces 85%

VIRGO TAROT

The Saintly One:

For most Virgos, sex is considered taboo. A sense of sanctity surrounds this sign. This doesn't mean they don't engage in it; on the contrary... but they prefer not to talk about it. Finally, Virgo appreciates comfort, even in a car, but with reclining seats, air conditioning, a stereo, and so on.

The Solitary One:

Sex is essential but not fundamental for sex in Virgos; they are very cerebral. Therefore, both men and women, if they don't find their soulmate, prefer to be alone. Typically, if they're not in the mood, they go with 'the Black Moon'... which means nothing, no sex tonight.

The Musician:

Nevertheless, there is a type that drives Virgo crazy: the Musician. This person knows how to play the right notes at the right time. Very changeable, Virgo needs someone who talks when they should talk and stays quiet when they should stay quiet. Difficult to find...

The Hidden Side:

On the surface, it may seem that Virgo has reached inner peace, but the trick lies in Self-gratification. Since they know their own bodies well, nobody else does. If they were to go blind, most blind people would be Virgos.

Libra - Air Sign -

Characteristics

You are characterized by Justice. Intelligent, intuitive, yet somewhat lazy, you possess a strong spirit of independence. Communicative and straightforward, you adapt to various situations effortlessly. As a Libra man, you are kind and gallant but also impulsive and somewhat restless. You find it challenging to put down roots, and your indecision can create an unstable balance. You're captivated by newness, beauty, and art. A refined gourmet, you enjoy cooking, hosting convivial dinners, and relishing the social scene. You embody the role of a peacemaker, advocating for peace and justice. In matters of love, you can be inconsistent, and men, in particular, may struggle with fidelity, but you are also deeply sensitive and willing to go to great lengths for friendship.

General Horoscope 2024

Opportunity Knocks!

Dear Libra friends, 2024 promises to be a year of significant opportunities and challenges. Here's what you can expect in the coming year.

You'll kick off 2024 with a positive energy boost and a fair share of luck on your side. This will be a favorable time to take on new challenges and pursue your goals with enthusiasm. Professionally, it will be a fruitful year thanks to Jupiter's transit in Aries, but remember to strike a balance between work and family.

However, early in the year, Saturn may test you with delays and financial matters. With your determination, you'll overcome these challenges. You'll continue to shine with your charming personality and intelligence, which will help you tackle challenges and impress others.

The second half of the year will be particularly favorable for your personal life. With direct Mars and active Venus, you'll find success in relationships and personal projects.

Towards the end of the year, Pluto's transit in Pisces will bring powerful transformations into your life. You'll feel excited and accomplished, but you may also face moments of uncertainty. Remember not to overly worry about temporary setbacks. Keep perspective and approach every situation with determination.

In summary, 2024 will be a year of ups and downs for you, Libra. With your ability to maintain balance and gracefully handle challenges, you'll achieve many extraordinary things. Keep your positivity and continue to be as charming as ever

Libra - Love Horoscope 2024

2024 starts with a burst of positivity for you, dear Libra friend! It's a perfect time to rekindle passion in your current relationship or start a new one. Think about romantic getaways or special moments with your partner. Approach any relationship issues with openness and maturity.

Spring brings further improvement to your love life. It's a fortunate period for singles, with the chance to meet someone special. Some may even find their "life partner." Remember to maintain an optimistic attitude despite occasional emotional fluctuations.

Summer might bring some ups and downs in relationships, but nothing that can't be overcome. Focus on open communication and emotional management. Avoid aggressive behaviors and work together with your partner to overcome obstacles.

Towards the end of the year, your love life will strengthen even further. You might even consider expanding your family. The key will be communication and mutual understanding.

Love and Relationship Tips:

Communicate Openly: Open communication is the key to a healthy relationship. Share your feelings with your partner.

Manage Emotions: Keep control over your emotions, even when things get intense. Patience and understanding will be crucial.

Solve Problems Together: Approach relationship challenges with maturity and work together to find solutions.

Stay Optimistic: Maintain a positive attitude about yourself and your love life. Self-confidence can lead to positive outcomes.

Family Planning: If you wish to expand your family, plan carefully and choose the right time.

2024 offers opportunities for growth in your relationships, Libra. Be open to love and reconciliation, manage challenges with maturity, and dedicate quality time to your partner. Open communication and mutual understanding will be crucial for the success of your relationships.

Libra - Finance Horoscope 2024

2024 looks promising for you, dear Libra! Right from the beginning of the year, with Mars turning direct, you'll see financial growth and development. It will be a period of smiles as your earnings increase.

Investments, such as those related to property or gold, will yield profits and wealth. Additionally, with the positive influence of Jupiter and Saturn, your financial situation will improve significantly. Some of you will achieve a more solid financial position. It will be a relief for those who were under pressure from loans or debts.

Savings Management:

Show your balanced side, Libra! Saturn's arrival in your sign might test your financial habits. Reflect on how you save or spend your money. Start saving early in the year, as this will help maintain financial stability, especially in the third quarter. Keep in mind that investments should be made carefully, and seek advice when necessary.

Career and Business Growth:

Are you ready to take a step forward in your financial career? Throughout the year, you'll experience steady growth. You might even find new opportunities to earn money. The second quarter will be particularly favorable, with possibilities for additional income from various sources. Don't be afraid to explore new opportunities or invest towards the end of the year.

Risk Reconciliation:

Financially, there will be moments of inner conflict, but other planets will help you overcome them. In the third quarter, you might face some financial challenges, but wise decisions will help you overcome them. Avoid excessive risks, but consider redeeming your short-term investments. It will be a year where financial wisdom pays off.

2024 promises financial prosperity for you, Libra. Maintain balance in your financial habits, start saving early, and be open to growth opportunities. This will be a year where your financial hard work bears fruit.

Libra - Career Horoscope 2024

2024 will bring challenges but also many opportunities in your career. While Saturn will test you from the start, this year looks promising for your profession, education, and business ventures. Professionals looking to take a break from ongoing projects will achieve positive results with dedication and determination. Of course, there will be obstacles along the way, but your resolutions and personal plans will increase your chances of achieving significant milestones and long-term success. Get ready for skill improvement, as there's room to grow.

Face Challenges with Determination:

Additionally, Mercury will play a significant role during the year. You might experience difficulties in your communication and decision-making abilities, which could impact your job performance, especially if you're seeking new employment or starting your career. Students may feel overwhelmed and low on energy. Those aiming for government roles will need extra commitment. However, once Mercury's influence subsides, you'll see things in a new light and can turn challenges into opportunities.

Opportunistic Approach to Business:

Businessmen and women will need to exhibit exceptional skills and techniques, particularly if they manage family businesses. 2024 is the perfect year to put your opportunistic approaches into practice and give it your all. Jupiter's positive influence will provide intelligence and willpower, so plan your initiatives carefully, especially in the second quarter. If you have entrepreneurial aspirations, this is the ideal phase to start new projects, either alone or in collaboration. Prepare for success!

Overcoming Obstacles:

However, towards the end of the year, you might experience some difficulties due to Pluto and Uranus' movements. These won't be insurmountable obstacles, but you'll need to be mindful of the people you work with, as they could negatively influence your professional reputation. Focus on self-improvement and personal growth rather than worrying excessively about what others think. Challenges will pass quickly.

This 2024 will be a year of growth, opportunity, and positive changes in your career, Libra. Maintain your determination and optimistic mindset, and you'll achieve the success you desire.

Libra - Family Horoscope 2024

2024 might feel like an emotional rollercoaster for your family and relationships. The rough road of the previous year will leave its mark on family matters. In the first half of the year, Mars will end its retrograde phase, helping you face challenges with courage and determination. Issues might arise between you and your parents, or you might have to deal with health-related concerns about them. However, there won't be severe disruptions in family peace overall.

The second half of the year brings good news, as Saturn and Jupiter collaborate to bring peace and harmony to your family. They will resolve ongoing tensions and contribute to creating an atmosphere of understanding among family members. It's essential not to hold back on addressing problems openly to avoid deep wounds.

For some of you, there will be good news in the form of a move or a change of residence. You might finally get the home you've always wanted or have the opportunity to relocate for professional reasons. This event will bring joy to the family but might create tensions between you and your siblings. Additionally, marital disputes due to financial issues might arise, but with the support of planetary transits and your supporters, you can overcome them together with your spouse.

Throughout the year, many of you will be ready to share exceptional news with your parents, bringing joy to their lives. However, in the last quarter, there might be ups and downs in the health of family members, especially among the younger ones, with possible anxiety-related issues. Some sibling conflicts might emerge due to the influence of Pluto and Uranus on emotions. Additionally, Saturn could cause delays in domestic matters, but these issues will be temporary and you'll face them with determination.

Remember, Libra, that open communication and mutual understanding are key to maintaining family stability. Face obstacles with courage, and in the end, harmony and joy will return to your family.

Libra - Health Horoscope 2024

2024 will test your health, but with care and determination, you can overcome any obstacles. Pluto and Uranus will serve as warnings for you, so it's important that those who are already unwell pay particular attention to their health.

Believe in therapy and medical practice and maintain a positive attitude. Don't allow pessimism to take over because Jupiter will be on your side, protecting you from injuries and illnesses.

In the second quarter of 2024, Libra natives will free themselves from persistent health issues such as bodily pain and mental fatigue. Those in good health will further improve their well-being, giving them the push to excel in other areas of life.

Saturn's influence will help you maintain a balanced and healthy lifestyle. Avoid poor eating habits and regularly practice yoga and/or meditation. These will protect you from pessimism and promote your long-term health. For elderly individuals with chronic illnesses, it's crucial to combat the fear of isolation by dedicating time to optimistic thoughts.

Saturn and Jupiter in your horoscope will bring positive thoughts and renewed energy, allowing you to achieve better results in your personal and professional life. You'll eliminate the thought of "I can't do it" and be driven by enthusiasm. In the third quarter, Venus will urge you to push your limits, maintaining your determination despite some health risks. Don't worry too much and do your best.

Towards the end of the year, you might feel physically drained, experiencing digestive and nervous issues. These could be related to stress and poor eating habits. Maintaining a balanced lifestyle will be crucial, as well as taking breaks for your long-term well-being.

Remember, even though the last months may seem challenging from a health perspective, optimism and stress management will be the keys to facing them successfully.

Couple Affinity

Him Libra

Libra - Aries: 71%

Libra - Taurus: 86%

Libra - Gemini: 88%

Libra - Cancer: 73%

Libra - Leo: 92%

Libra - Virgo: 69%

Libra - Libra: 73%

Libra - Scorpio: 78%

Libra - Sagittarius: 75%

Libra - Capricorn: 60%

Libra - Aquarius: 63%

Libra - Pisces: 69%

Couple Affinity

Her Libra

Libra - Aries: 86%

Libra - Taurus: 88%

Libra - Gemini: 68%

Libra - Cancer: 69%

Libra - Leo: 89%

Libra - Virgo: 69%

Libra - Libra: 73%

Libra - Scorpio: 68%

Libra - Sagittarius: 69%

Libra - Capricorn: 83%

Libra - Aquarius: 79%

Libra - Pisces: 75%

Libra Tarot

The Artist:

Libra is fundamentally an artist. You have a knack for bringing out your partner's hidden talents. You add that touch that revives everything. Even when it comes to sex, you're creative and always find new ways to provide unexpected pleasure. With Libra, sex is an art that's never vulgar.

The Collector:

Being an artist, Libra enjoys building their collection. They have experiences with very different partners because they don't just focus on appearances but look beyond. Often, Libra becomes fascinated by their work, passions, and even dreams. Because Libra is a dreamer.

The Magician:

Libra has that certain "je ne sais quoi" that's captivating, you know... But the strangest thing is that at times, they can appear truly magical. They naturally create an atmosphere where even sex becomes something special. In bed, they drive their partner wild, but unfortunately, they also get bored too easily.

The Hidden Side:

A great lover, a sex machine, Libra is always at the center of attention, so Betrayal, which is in their nature, remains a constant threat throughout the relationship. For Libra, cheating is normal, but being cheated on is not, causing them to lose important people and opportunities.

Scorpio- Water Sign –

Characteristics

You are characterized by alliances. Decisive, you, Scorpio, don't do things halfway: it's either black or white. You have strong likes or irreversible dislikes. In this sign, strengths and weaknesses are evenly divided. If someone wrongs you, you remember it forever, and when the time is right, you know how to seek revenge. Resourceful and inventive, you are sharp as a tack. Proud and easily irritable, you have a temper that can lead to confrontations. Primarily an artist in how you color your life, at times, you may go through identity crises. Hidden within you is a desire for recognition. Passionate, it's easy for you to become obsessively attached to someone. Jealous and possessive, you shoot down anyone you consider a potential rival. Scorpio does not like to lose, especially in love.

General Horoscope 2024

If you always do the same things...

You will always get the same results.

Dear Scorpios, 2024 will bring significant changes in your perceptions and opportunities in your life. It will be a year where the stars will compel you to see things in a different light, especially in your personal relationships.

This change will be driven by the planet Mars, your ruling planet, which will end its retrograde period in the early first quarter. Saturn, at the same time, will caution you to be mindful of your professional life. But fear not, for Jupiter will be by your side until the third quarter of the year, bringing blessings to you and your family. So, get ready to see your viewpoints evolve and embrace new perspectives.

In the second half of the year, financial opportunities will knock on your door, but be cautious when Venus goes into combustion. Make the most of this favorable period to improve your financial situation.

Additionally, there might be a shift in your personal life. If you're looking for new responsibilities or a new relationship, you'll be ready to commit. If you're already in a relationship, you'll discover a more supportive side of your partner, deepening your bond. However, be aware of potential health challenges due to the influence of the planet Mercury, especially in the last quarter of 2024. Take care of yourself and maintain good mental and physical health.

2024 promises new perspectives and opportunities for you, Scorpio. It will be a year of personal growth and relationship development. Face challenges with optimism and prepare for a year of significant changes.

Scorpio Love Horoscope 2024

2024 will bring important changes in the dynamics of your love and personal relationships. It will be a year where you discover new aspects of your relationships and experience significant personal growth.

New Relationship Perspectives:

2024 will start with an entirely new perspective on your romantic relationships. Thanks to the influence of the planet Mars, you will see things differently and may feel the need to explore new horizons. Some of you might even make significant decisions about your initial relationships. It will be a period of self-reflection and personal growth.

Family Matters:

Family dynamics will be in the spotlight in the first half of the year. You might experience tensions or conflicts with older family members, possibly related to professional matters. It's important to address these challenges calmly and patiently. Keep in mind that these difficulties will resolve as the influence of Saturn and Jupiter brings harmony back in the second quarter. Patience and open communication will be key to resolving family issues.

Love and Personal Relationships:

Your personal relationships will take center stage throughout the year. For singles, the second quarter will be a favorable time to start new relationships or deepen existing ones. You'll feel more confident and communicative, making it easier to connect with others.

Growth in Existing Relationships:

For those already in a relationship, 2024 will bring opportunities for growth. You might decide to take your relationship to the next level, such as engagement or cohabitation. It will also be a year when you can rely on your partner's support in facing personal and professional challenges. Communication will be crucial to strengthening your bond with your partner.

Marriage and Long-Term Commitments:

Couples considering marriage might receive proposals or make significant decisions towards the end of the year. The stars favor long-term commitments and marital life plans. Make sure to pay attention to details and involve your family in the planning process.

2024 will be a year of growth, discovery, and change in your romantic and family relationships. It's essential to be open to new perspectives and communicate openly with your loved ones. Patience and understanding will be the keys to facing challenges and seizing opportunities throughout the year.

Scorpio Finance Horoscope 2024

2024 promises to bring new financial opportunities and growth for you, although you may have to face some challenges along the way.

Savings Management:

This year, it's essential to be cautious in managing your savings and investments. Saturn will continue to exert its influence, encouraging you to plan carefully and make wise financial decisions. Avoid risky investments and aim to maintain a solid financial foundation. Start early in the year by setting aside a portion of your earnings to handle potential unexpected expenses.

Career and Business Growth:

Your career and financial opportunities will see steady growth throughout 2024. Jupiter will bless you with financial gains, especially in the first half of the year. Be open to new projects and collaborations as they can bring significant benefits. However, pay attention to your personal finances and plan carefully, especially in the second quarter when Mercury may bring some challenges.

Reconciliation with Risks:

While Pluto and Uranus may bring inner conflicts and complex situations, it's essential not to be overwhelmed by pressure. Make financial decisions calmly and carefully consider your options. Avoid taking excessive risks, but don't be afraid to explore new opportunities. Maintain an optimistic outlook and seek creative solutions to overcome challenges.

2024 will be a year where you can leverage financial opportunities that come your way. Maintain a prudent approach and plan your financial moves carefully. With dedication and attention, you can achieve your financial goals and create a solid foundation for the future.

Scorpio Career Horoscope 2024

2024 begins with Saturn testing your patience and self-control in your career. You may even feel lost or uncomfortable in your work environment. Achieving your professional goals may seem like a challenge. It's essential to take precautions, identify your weaknesses, and improve your skills to successfully navigate work-related challenges.

Opportunities for Newcomers:

In the second half of the year, the planets Jupiter and Saturn will be favorable for newcomers in the professional world. Students seeking internships or freelance work can plan to do so during this period. Concentration and dedication will be required, but success is attainable.

Energetic Fluctuations:

With Pluto and Uranus influencing your horoscope, you may experience energy highs and lows. This could affect your professional life and studies. However, some individuals in technical fields may receive promotions or recognition at work.

Business Opportunities:

If you are involved in a family business or entrepreneurial endeavor, 2024 may bring offers to expand your initiatives. The major breakthrough will come in the third quarter, with Jupiter and Mercury improving your communication skills and fostering favorable collaborations. However, be cautious about sharing company secrets.

Success in International Business:

The last quarter of 2024 could bring success and profits in business, with international opportunities on the horizon. Make sure to choose the right time to take advantage of these opportunities and protect your interests.

Support for Individual Initiatives:

If you're starting a small business or a startup, you'll receive support from your parents and others. Venus's combustion will help you manage business finances, but be cautious about making hasty decisions due to the impulsive energy brought by Pluto.

2024 will bring both challenges and opportunities in your career. The key to success will be self-improvement, careful planning, and wise management of opportunities. Be open to new opportunities and work diligently to achieve your professional goals.

Scorpio Family Horoscope 2024

2024 will begin with some challenges in family dynamics, as seen in 2023. With Saturn's transit in Aquarius in the first quarter, you may experience ups and downs in your home. Conflicts with older family members, perhaps related to professional reasons, may arise. It's essential to address these challenges calmly and patiently. Keep in mind that these difficulties will resolve in the second quarter, thanks to the positive influences of Jupiter and Saturn.

Family Growth and Happiness:

The arrival of Jupiter will bring a burst of positive energy and happiness to your family. Throughout 2024, there may be changes or modifications in your family, such as a sibling changing residence. While this could cause some temporary turbulence, thanks to the blessings of Jupiter and Saturn, you'll overcome these challenges without significant issues.

Grandparents' Health and Children's Success:

In the last quarter, there may be health issues among your grandparents. It will be essential to pay attention to their health and ensure they receive the care they need. Meanwhile, Scorpio children will excel in their activities and studies, enjoying good health.

Affectionate Moments:

2024 will bring affectionate moments and family harmony, provided you listen to yourself and show patience towards your family members. Patience will be crucial in resolving any family disputes. The planet Venus will support you in this effort.

Preparation for Challenges:

Towards the end of the year, some challenges related to children may arise, but overall, 2024 promises to be a pleasant year for Scorpio individuals.

2024 will bring some family challenges at the beginning, but these will resolve over time thanks to your patience. The year also promises moments of growth, happiness, and family success. It's important to pay attention to grandparents' health and support children in their growth and goals. Maintain open and affectionate communication with family members to create an atmosphere of harmony and love.

Scorpio Health Horoscope 2024

2024 will bring relief for Scorpio natives, with the possibility of recovering from persistent illnesses and other health issues from the previous year. From the beginning of the year, with Mars ending its retrograde period in the first quarter, your immunity will be strong, and you'll enjoy a period of relaxation that contributes to your overall well-being.

Lifestyle Improvements:

Saturn will continue to exert pressure for you to make lifestyle improvements right from the beginning of the year. It's important to heed these signals and make necessary changes for a healthier life.

Mid-Year Challenges:

Around the middle of the year, you may face some health challenges, especially during the months when Venus is in retrograde position. This could make you more vulnerable and affect your energy levels, potentially impacting your professional life. It's crucial to pay attention to your health, especially if you have immunity issues or digestive system-related disorders. Following a healthy diet and maintaining a balanced lifestyle will be essential.

Pregnancy Health:

For Scorpio women expecting to bring new life into the world, the horoscope indicates good health during pregnancy.

Children and External Influences:

For Scorpio children, there may be some challenges related to external influences or viral illnesses in the first half of the year. It will be essential to provide them with the necessary care to overcome these difficult times.

Weight Loss and Body Shaping:

Those who have decided to lose weight or engage in body shaping may face some challenges when Pluto influences in the last quarter of the year. However, other planets will be there to support you and keep your motivation high.

Positive Mindset:

For Scorpio individuals in good health, 2024 promises continuous improvement in your daily routine. It's essential to create healthy habits in your lifestyle and maintain a positive mindset. The year will generally be favorable both mentally and physically. Keep in mind that excessive worry could lead to moments of discomfort, but thanks to Jupiter's influence, you'll be encouraged to overcome any medical challenges.

2024 will bring improvements in your health, with strong immunity and the possibility of recovery from persistent illnesses. It's crucial to maintain a healthy lifestyle and address any health challenges with patience and care. Maintain a positive mindset and listen to your body's signals to enjoy a year of health and well-being.

Couple Affinity

Him Scorpio

Scorpio - Aries 71%

Scorpio - Taurus 91%

Scorpio - Gemini 89%

Scorpio - Cancer 78%

Scorpio - Leo 78%

Scorpio - Virgo 73%

Scorpio - Libra 68%

Scorpio - Scorpio 90%

Scorpio - Sagittarius 65%

Scorpio - Capricorn 66%

Scorpio - Aquarius 59%

Scorpio - Pisces 61%

Couple Affinity

Her Scorpio

Scorpio - Aries 73%

Scorpio - Taurus 80%

Scorpio - Gemini 79%

Scorpio - Cancer 79%

Scorpio - Leo 56%

Scorpio - Virgo 76%

Scorpio - Libra 78%

Scorpio - Scorpio 90%

Scorpio - Sagittarius 58%

Scorpio - Capricorn 77%

Scorpio - Aquarius 67%

Scorpio - Pisces 89%

SCORPIO TAROT

The Genius: Scorpio is undoubtedly a genius, which sets them a step above others. Sex is fundamental to them in all its forms and with all its surrogates. Determined, especially Scorpio men have women who would follow them blindly. Not all, though.

The Vampire: Scorpio is a vampire, a sucker, in the sense that they always seek to extract the essence, leaving others with the husk. Despite the initial fear, you can be pleasantly surprised. You are one of the few signs that use their heads even in sex.

The Poet: One can be captivated listening to a Scorpio. They are born poets, declaiming their verses, adapting them to whomever they have in front of them. So enchanting and invasive that they sting a person without them realizing it. When they do realize it, it's already too late.

The Hidden Side: Scorpio has a weakness, Gluttony: in sex, they are never satisfied, always wanting more. This can lead them to be captured eventually. Whoever approaches the fire too closely risks getting burned, and that's what can happen to Scorpio. What a pity.

Sagittarius - Fire Sign –

Characteristics

I Think. You're the opinionator. Sociable, loyal, you exude energy from every pore. You're very straightforward but try to have your opinion prevail over others. You always want the last word. Versatile, you have a natural disregard for danger. Despite this, sometimes you're negative and see everything in a negative light. You love nature in all its forms. You, Sagittarius, like to share walks, sunshine, the sea, the mountains, and friends with your partner. You have above-average intelligence. Sometimes you're loved, and at other times, hated. You get emotional easily and have a good dose of imagination. In love, you're exuberant and very fiery. It's not about what's beautiful, but what you like ... and Sagittarius "likes."

General Horoscope 2024

A Year to Fall in Love... Finally

2024 will bring a great dose of optimism into your life, Sagittarius. The positive approach to life that you bring at the beginning of the year will be crucial for your future success. You will be able to face challenges with determination and hard work, which will positively reflect on your career. The stars indicate that this will be a favorable year for those seeking opportunities in government jobs, with Venus and Jupiter bringing positivity to finances in the first half of the year.

Love and Relationships

2024 will be a favorable year for your romantic relationships. The influence of Venus in your natal chart will push you to seek and establish romantic connections. Even if you are more reserved by nature, you will feel the urge to socialize and meet people of the opposite sex. Predictions indicate that you will not be disappointed; in fact, you can expect to start new romantic relationships from the beginning of the year and expand your social circle throughout the year.

Finances and Expenses

While there will be positivity in your finances thanks to Venus and Jupiter in the first half of the year, it is important to be careful with expenses. Pluto and Uranus could bring financial instability, so it is advisable to manage your money and investments carefully in 2024.

Education and Progress

Jupiter will initially provide a positive boost to your education and progress in 2024. However, the presence of Saturn after the first quarter could make it difficult to maintain this momentum. You will need to make an extra effort to achieve your educational goals and combat any frustration that may arise.

Health and Well-being

Your health and physical fitness will be favored thanks to Jupiter in 2024. However, pay attention to an unhealthy diet that could cause fatigue in the early months of the year. Try to adopt a healthier and more active lifestyle to maintain your well-being. Occasional work-related tensions could affect your health, so avoid stress and focus on your mental health.

2024 will be a year of optimism, opportunities, and growth for you, Sagittarius. Make the most of the opportunities that arise in your career and personal relationships, wisely manage your finances, persist in your educational goals, and pay attention to your well-being. With the right approach, you can face any challenges that 2024 may bring and thrive in all aspects of your life.

Sagittarius Love Horoscope 2024

You are known to be cautious when it comes to love and relationships, Sagittarius, but 2024 will lead you to seek love with greater fervor thanks to the influence of Venus in your horoscope. At the beginning of the year, you will have the opportunity to meet interesting people with whom to share affectionate bonds. However, for those who are already in a relationship, Mars could bring disputes and even the risk of interference from third parties. It will be important to stay calm, control anger, and have patience in love.

Proposals and Revelations

The first quarter of the year is the ideal time to propose marriage or reveal your love story to your parents. The positive influence of Venus will ensure their support. For those who wish to get married, the end of the year will be the most suitable time. If you want to have a child, the first quarter will be highly favorable, but you may need to keep your love life secret in the early months of the year if you plan to reveal it to your family.

Singles Looking for Love

Single Sagittarians will feel a push to seek love in 2024 thanks to the energy of Venus. January could be a memorable month to meet someone special, with the peak of Venus's energy in February. However, avoid rushing into serious commitments, as Affinity could be an issue later in the year.

Married Couples and Relationships

Married couples will enjoy renewed intimacy throughout the year thanks to the influence of Venus. Plan trips or special experiences with your spouse to strengthen your bond. However, pay attention to a lack of attention in the second half of the year when your partner may complain. Make an effort to be more expressive and attentive during this time.

Challenging Moments

In the second half of the year, you may experience some challenges in your love life. Avoid unnecessary confrontations and work to maintain mutual understanding. In the month of August, be aware of possible disappointments in the marriage and make a special effort to make your partner happy.

Marriages and Engagements

If you plan to get married in 2024, the last quarter of the year will be the best time. This period will be highly favorable for proposals and engagements. However, be cautious in August, as it could bring disappointments in marital relationships.

2024 will be a year when Sagittarius is more open to love and relationships. It will be important to stay calm during challenges and work to maintain a strong bond with your partner. If you are single, you may find love unexpectedly, but take your time to get to know the person better. Overall, 2024 will bring opportunities and growth in your romantic and emotional relationships.

Sagittarius Career Horoscope 2024

The Sagittarius horoscope predicts many good career opportunities coming your way in 2024. In fact, this year, you will be fortunate to find a job based on your skills. This will boost your confidence and inspire you to work harder. The strong presence of Jupiter in the Sagittarius horoscope for 2024 will aid business growth after April 2024. However, the first few months of 2024 are not the best for business expansion or growth. Therefore, it is advisable to make informed decisions and take minimal risks regarding your business during this period.

The combined effect of Venus, Mercury, and Jupiter in the Sagittarius horoscope for 2024 indicates stronger possibilities than ever of getting a raise or even a promotion in 2024. The promotion, therefore, will bring much-needed financial benefits after the month of March. However, there may also be strong competition, which could test your mental well-being. In the early months of 2024, newcomers will also have many opportunities to find the job they are looking for. Furthermore, if you are looking for a change, April is the perfect time to change jobs according to the Sagittarius horoscope for 2024.

2024 is the year of realization for Sagittarius. Therefore, as the year progresses (during the second half), you will have a strong urge to make plans to try new things in life. The drive may make you doubt your current career prospects, and you may appear dissatisfied.

Furthermore, you will realize that you are more capable, and this could be the euphoria that drives you to make changes in life or even adopt a secondary hustle. In the second half, businessmen will be able to strengthen their position in the market as Mercury and Jupiter favor them. If you feel that your hard work is not paying off, the feeling will change in the second half of the year.

During the last quarter of the year, you may have the opportunity to travel for various work-related reasons.

The presence of Venus during this period will aid career growth at a normal pace. However, around the month of October, you need to be a bit cautious in the office as some of your colleagues may cause you serious problems. Overall, the planets will keep you motivated to work hard in 2024.

Sagittarius Finance Horoscope 2024

2024 brings good news for Sagittarius' financial health, with the Moon positively influencing your physical and mental health. However, you will need to pay particular attention to your mental health, especially in the second half of the year when unexpected challenges may arise. Investing in your mental health will be crucial to maintaining balance.

Physical Health

In the first three months of 2024, Saturn transits into Pisces, favoring good health. This period may bring improvements for those who have faced health issues. Thanks to the strong influence of Jupiter in your natal chart, the likelihood of serious health problems is low, allowing you to enjoy good physical health.

Children's Health

Your children may experience some health issues during and after April 2024 due to the effects of Jupiter and Pluto. It will be important to take care of your children during this period, encouraging a healthy lifestyle and physical activity. Provide them with a balanced diet to maintain their health.

Areas of Focus:

In 2024, pay particular attention to the health of your eyes and stomach. Have regular eye check-ups to detect any problems in a timely manner. Avoid excessive consumption of junk food and strive to maintain a balanced diet to preserve stomach health.

Mental Health

Mental health will be a point of focus in 2024, especially in the second half of the year. If you encounter challenges or difficulties, do not hesitate to seek professional support or engage in activities that help you manage stress and anxiety. Traveling and connecting with nature can have a positive effect on your mental health.

Pregnancy and Maternity

For pregnant Sagittarius women, it is important to avoid stress and find comfort in nature. The month of November 2024 may require special attention to health during pregnancy. Consider planning a honeymoon or a relaxing break for comfort and well-being.

2024 offers opportunities for good physical health, but it requires attention to mental health and specific areas such as eyes and stomach. Maintain a healthy lifestyle, pay attention to your diet, and find ways to manage stress. Taking care of the health of your children and pregnant women will be essential during the year.

Sagittarius Family Horoscope 2024

2024 will bring a series of changes and challenges in the family sphere for Sagittarius. It will be a year in which you will need to manage family dynamics with wisdom and patience. However, there will also be moments of joy, growth, and strengthening of family bonds.

Family Relationships

At the beginning of the year, you may experience some tensions or disagreements within your family. The presence of Saturn could test your patience and communication skills with family members. It is important to address conflicts constructively and seek solutions through dialogue. Over time, family relationships will strengthen thanks to your dedication to maintaining harmony.

Family Changes

In the second half of the year, you may witness significant changes within your family. These changes could include moves, weddings, births, or other significant events. It is essential to be flexible and adaptable in the face of these transitions and offer your support to family members in need.

Parents and Elderly Relatives

Take care of your parents and elderly relatives, especially during times when they may face health issues. Your presence and support will be valuable to them. Make sure to listen to their needs and ensure they receive the assistance they require.

Relationships with Children

If you have children, 2024 will be a year in which you can establish deeper connections with them. Dedicate quality time to your family and actively participate in your children's growth and development.

Quality Family Time

Plan special family moments, such as vacations or gatherings, to strengthen bonds and create lasting memories. Sagittarius has an adventurous nature, so look for activities that all family members can enjoy and share.

Family Education

Family education and growth will be at the forefront in 2024. Try to create a positive learning environment within the family, where everyone can share their experiences and learn from each other.

2024 will bring changes and challenges in the family sphere for Sagittarius, but also opportunities to strengthen bonds and create meaningful moments with your loved ones. Communication, patience, and mutual support will be crucial for navigating family dynamics during the year.

Sagittarius Health Horoscope 2024

2024 brings good news for Sagittarius' health, with the Moon positively influencing your physical and mental well-being. However, you will need to pay particular attention to your mental health, especially in the second half of the year when unexpected challenges may arise. Investing in your mental health will be crucial to maintaining balance.

Physical Health

In the first three months of 2024, Saturn transits into Pisces, favoring good health. This period may bring improvements for those who have faced health issues. Thanks to the strong influence of Jupiter in your natal chart, the likelihood of serious health problems is low, allowing you to enjoy good physical health.

Children's Health

Your children may experience some health issues during and after April 2024 due to the effects of Jupiter and Pluto. It will be important to take care of your children during this period, encouraging a healthy lifestyle and physical activity. Provide them with a balanced diet to maintain their health.

Areas of Focus:

In 2024, pay particular attention to the health of your eyes and stomach. Have regular eye check-ups to detect any problems in a timely manner. Avoid excessive consumption of junk food and strive to maintain a balanced diet to preserve stomach health.

Mental Health

Mental health will be a point of focus in 2024, especially in the second half of the year. If you encounter challenges or difficulties, do not hesitate to seek professional support or engage in activities that help you manage stress and anxiety. Traveling and connecting with nature can have a positive effect on your mental health.

Pregnancy and Maternity

For pregnant Sagittarius women, it is important to avoid stress and find comfort in nature. The month of November 2024 may require special attention to health during pregnancy. Consider planning a honeymoon or a relaxing break for comfort and well-being.

2024 offers opportunities for good physical health, but it requires attention to mental health and specific areas such as eyes and stomach. Maintain a healthy lifestyle, pay attention to your diet, and find ways to manage stress. Taking care of the health of your children and pregnant women will be essential during the year.

Affinity of Couples

Him Sagittarius

Sagittarius - Aries 76%

Sagittarius - Taurus 81%

Sagittarius - Gemini 83%

Sagittarius - Cancer 79%

Sagittarius - Leo 83%

Sagittarius - Virgo 59%

Sagittarius - Libra 69%

Sagittarius - Scorpio 58%

Sagittarius - Sagittarius 75%

Sagittarius - Capricorn 63%

Sagittarius - Aquarius 84%

Sagittarius - Pisces 71%

Affinity of Couples

Her Sagittarius

Sagittarius - Aries 81%

Sagittarius - Taurus 83%

Sagittarius - Gemini 78%

Sagittarius - Cancer 84%

Sagittarius - Leo 75%

Sagittarius - Virgo 63%

Sagittarius - Libra 75%

Sagittarius - Scorpio 65%

Sagittarius - Sagittarius 75%

Sagittarius - Capricorn 76%

Sagittarius - Aquarius 83%

Sagittarius - Pisces 78%

Sagittarius Tarot

The Pirate:

Sagittarius likes to be a bit of a Pirate and a bit of a Lord. Their ideal is to be a wild person on a deserted island, where you eat, drink, and have sex. It's the Tarzan type: take, open, and enjoy! But this shouldn't translate into a quickie in the nightclub restroom. Why? Because it would lose its poetic charm... or not.

The Nymphomaniac:

Men have a fiery character, but Sagittarius women are truly demanding. They're not of the "first time's good" type; it has to be good the second, third, and so on. Tireless to the point of seeming like nymphomaniacs. You might hear them say, "You wanted the bicycle? Well, now pedal."

The Sadist:

Sagittarius doesn't hold back, but sometimes they go overboard. They don't do it out of malice, but sometimes they can seem sadistic. They take erotic games to the extreme. It's a bit like when you string a bow to shoot an arrow as far as possible. However, be careful not to break the string.

The Hidden Side:

If the woman is a bit of a nymphomaniac, the man is a bit of a maniac. Sagittarians have a one-track mind. As a song says, before and after meals, morning, afternoon, and evening. But at night? Yes, even at night. To a good listener, few words are needed, but many deeds. Or put simply: deeds, not words.

Capricorn - Earth Sign –

Characteristics:

You are characterized by morals and rules. Ambitious, you have a character that can sometimes seem cold; this is due to your seriousness and caution. You tend to be pessimistic and fear failure. You tend to isolate yourself, disliking crowds, crowds, and anything that puts you in question. You know well that being almost devoid of humor, you cannot stand jokes and mediocre people, whom you treat with condescension. Filled with a great spirit of sacrifice, you, Capricorn, are a marathon runner: when others run out of strength, you put in an extra gear and reach the finish line first. You are diplomatic and very controlled, even in bed, where it seems you do it out of duty. In this field, you are hard to warm up, but once you get started, you perform well and are very reliable.

General Horoscope 2024:

New Year - New You

2024 will bring significant changes in the life of Capricorn. You are known for being reserved, but this year, openness and communication will be essential to overcome challenges. Mars may bring obstacles and issues in the first quarter, but Mercury will intervene to improve the situation. Expressing your thoughts and feelings will help you gain the support of those around you.

Career and Work:

Jupiter's position will favor your finances in 2024, but Saturn may hinder your path. Asking for help and communicating your problems will be crucial to overcoming financial challenges. This will not only improve your financial situation but also strengthen your personal and professional connections.

Love and Relationships:

Venus and Pluto will have a complex impact on your love life. Venus will help clarify your feelings about romantic matters, but Pluto may bring doubts and confusion. The key to overcoming this challenge is open and honest communication with your partner or potential partner. Expressing your feelings will help you overcome any obstacles.

Health:

Your health may have its ups and downs in 2024, but overall, you will have the opportunity to face challenges successfully. Pay attention to your mental health, especially in the second half of the year, and seek activities that help you manage stress and anxiety.

Remember to communicate your feelings with others, as this will have a positive impact on your health.

2024 requires Capricorn to open up more and communicate with others to overcome challenges and get the necessary support. In both your career and personal relationships, communication will be fundamental to success.

Capricorn Love Horoscope 2024:

2024 will bring a series of ups and downs in relationships for Capricorn. Communication will be crucial to overcoming challenges and ensuring success in romantic relationships.

Couples and Long-term Relationships:

Couples may face disagreements in the first half of the year. It's essential to address communication issues and work together to overcome them. Capricorns in long-term relationships will need to make important decisions about the future. Expressing true feelings and working on communication will help strengthen the relationship. While there may be difficulties, open communication will lead to issue resolution.

Singles and Dating:

Singles may encounter a new potential partner during the year. It's essential to take the time to understand their needs and desires before committing to a relationship. Communication will be crucial to avoiding misunderstandings and Affinity issues. The second half of the year will favor love stories, but communication will remain a key element for success.

Reconciliation:

If you intend to seek reconciliation with an ex-partner, the end of the year will be a favorable time to do so. The importance of honest communication and openness about feelings will be crucial to resolving issues and building a stronger relationship.

Marriage and Family:

2024 will be a good time for married Capricorns to plan to start a family. However, there may be disagreements and family responsibilities to manage in the second half of the year. Patient and open communication with your spouse will be essential to overcome these obstacles. Married couples may also consider new professional opportunities together.

Toxic Situations:

Those in toxic situations or relationships will experience better times in the second half of the year. Reconciliation or improvement of relationships will be possible, but it will be necessary to gather strength and seek the support of trusted individuals.

2024 for Capricorn in love will be characterized by challenges and opportunities. Open and honest communication will be the key to overcoming difficulties and building stronger romantic relationships.

Capricorn Finance Horoscope 2024:

2024 will be a year in which Capricorn will see financial improvements but must be cautious and prudent in financial decisions. Investments and real estate transactions will be particularly profitable.

Investments and Real Estate:

For financially savvy individuals, 2024 promises opportunities for success. Real estate investments and the sale of old properties will be advantageous, yielding significant profits. It's essential to pay attention to all details and involve trusted individuals in handling these matters. Investments in the last quarter will be particularly profitable.

Loan Sector:

Those working in the loan sector may face some financial management challenges by mid-year. While situations may be manageable, inattention can lead to problems. It's advisable to pay attention to details and deadlines.

Legal Involvement:

Some Capricorns may conclude legal matters related to money in 2024. Old connections may reconnect and offer financial assistance in the future.

Wealth and Fortune:

In the third quarter of 2024, opportunities for wealth and fortune will come your way. However, you may have to face some minor financial difficulties in certain areas. Short-term investments and considering entering SIPs or liquid funds will be useful strategies. Family members may contribute to your financial gains.

Spending and Savings:

2024 will be a good time to manage expenses, but it's important to be cautious. While you can enjoy some leisure time and make purchases for yourself and your loved ones, it's crucial to maintain savings for any emergencies that may arise in the second quarter.

Jewelry and Gemstones:

Women involved in jewelry and gemstones will see significant financial benefits in 2024. However, it's important to have a solid savings strategy, even as earnings increase.

Ancestral Properties and Family Involvement:

Ancestral properties and family involvement could influence the financial situation. Ensure you manage these matters prudently and maintain confidentiality when necessary.

2024 will bring financial opportunities for Capricorn, but it will also require attention, planning, and prudence in financial decisions. Real estate investments, wise investments, and careful expense management will be key to financial success throughout the year.

Capricorn Career Horoscope 2024:

2024 will be a year of growth and success for Capricorn in their careers. Your dedication to hard work and clear vision will help you achieve new levels of professional accomplishment. Both creative professionals and those aspiring to government jobs will find opportunities to advance.

Creative Professionals:

If you are involved in creative professions, you will be highly valued in 2024. Your understanding of the work will improve, allowing you to bring forward innovative ideas and stand out in your field.

Government Workers:

Capricorns involved in government jobs or aspiring to such positions may face challenges along the way. However, your commitment and positive attitude will help you overcome any obstacles. Results may not come until the end of the year, but your hard work will ultimately bear fruit.

Professional Relationships:

The second half of the year will be a time to showcase your abilities to your colleagues. Focus on your work and try to avoid office politics or hallway gossip. Partnerships may bring financial benefits and an improved professional reputation. If you work in the textile industry, you may consider new collaborations.

Mental Resilience:

Changes in planetary positions in the third quarter could bring doubts about your abilities. Avoid being influenced by negative people or those who are not genuinely interested in your success. Maintain self-confidence and seek support when needed.

Students:

Capricorn students may face challenges in studying and concentrating. However, don't get discouraged, as things will take a positive turn toward the end of the year. You will be able to overcome significant exams, obtain scholarships, or be admitted to prestigious colleges. Organize yourself well and be aware of the value of your time and effort. Professional counseling may be helpful if you feel stuck in your career.

2024 will be a year of professional growth and success for Capricorn. Your dedication, clear vision, and positive attitude will lead you to new levels of accomplishment. Whether you are a creative professional, a government worker, or a student, there will be opportunities for growth and improvement along the way.

Capricorn - Family Horoscope 2024:

In 2024, it's essential for you to show your love and appreciation for your family, but it's equally important to make them understand your ideologies and opinions. This will help create a positive mindset within your family and encourage your loved ones to make independent choices.

Sibling Relationships:

In the first half of the year, there may be sparks between you and your siblings, especially if they are younger than you. Be patient and try to resolve disputes through dialogue. Open communication and active listening will help overcome tensions.

Parent-Child Relationships:

Relationships with your parents may go through a phase of disagreements. In particular, Capricorn fathers may face negative opinions from their fathers. Try to maintain open communication with your parents and help them understand your point of view.

Health of Capricorn Women:

Capricorn women may face health challenges due to the workload and stress of balancing professional and personal life. You may feel tired and emotionally fluctuating. Make sure to take care of yourself and strive to find a balance between work and well-being.

Marital Relationships:

Married Capricorn women may experience disagreements with their in-laws or older family members. However, by the end of the year, things will take a positive turn with opportunities for travel. A family vacation can strengthen family bonds and benefit everyone.

Elderly Family Members:

Elderly family members may embark on a pilgrimage, which could bring them inner peace. However, there may be disputes or discussions due to interference from relatives. It's essential to openly discuss with family members to resolve any conflicts.

Financial Issues:

In the first quarter of 2024, financial issues and family disputes may arise. Ensure you take necessary steps to protect your family's financial reputation. Be cautious of individuals who may seek to harm your financial situation.

Children in the Family:

Children in the family will achieve positive results in their activities, but their behavior may be challenging to manage. Be patient and try to establish effective communication with them. In the second half of the year, there may be good news about a new family member, both for couples expecting a child and for singles finding a suitable partner.

2024 will bring challenges and opportunities in Capricorn's family relationships. Open communication, mutual understanding, and patience will be key to overcoming difficulties and strengthening family bonds.

Capricorn - Health Horoscope 2024:

In 2024, it's crucial for you to pay attention to your health and overall well-being. The year may begin with some challenges, but you can effectively manage them by taking the right precautions.

Express Your Feelings:

Remember how important it is to express your feelings rather than keeping everything inside. This will help reduce stress and mental tensions. If you need medical assistance, don't hesitate to seek it promptly.

Digestive Issues:

In the first quarter of the year, you may experience digestive issues due to an unhealthy diet. Avoid harmful foods and strive to follow a balanced diet to improve your digestive health.

Children and School Stress:

Children may face irritations and stress related to their studies. Ensure they take regular breaks and seek support from their teachers or friends if necessary. Avoid overburdening children with excessive expectations.

Health Improvements:

Around the third quarter of 2024, both men and women Capricorn will enjoy better health. Even those with health issues will see significant improvements. Continue to pay attention to your diet and lifestyle.

Health of Elderly Family Members:

Elderly family members may experience knee pain and back discomfort with the change of seasons. Activities like yoga and light physical exercise can help manage these issues. Spending time with the family will contribute to their overall well-being.

Long-Term Health Solutions:

If you are seeking long-term health solutions, the fourth quarter of 2024 may be a favorable time. Patience will be essential, but you will see significant improvements in your energy and vitality.

Anxiety and Stress:

Unnecessary anxiety could be a problem for many people during the year, especially for professionals under a heavy workload. Learn to manage stress healthily by taking breaks when needed and engaging in relaxing activities.

Health of Capricorn Women:

Capricorn women should pay particular attention to managing work and personal life. This is important for pregnant women as well. Maintain a well-structured schedule to ensure your well-being.

2024 may present some health challenges, but with proper wellness management, a balanced diet, and seeking medical assistance when necessary, you can face the year with improved health and vitality. Don't neglect your mental health and strive to find healthy ways to manage stress.

Couple Affinity

Him Capricorn

Capricorn - Aries 58%

Capricorn - Taurus 66%

Capricorn - Gemini 69%

Capricorn - Cancer 71%

Capricorn - Leo 80%

Capricorn - Virgo 78%

Capricorn - Libra 83%

Capricorn - Scorpio 77%

Capricorn - Sagittarius 76%

Capricorn – Capricorn 81%

Capricorn - Aquarius 68%

Capricorn - Pisces 69%

Couple Affinity

Her Capricorn

Capricorn - Aries 67%

Capricorn - Taurus 75%

Capricorn - Gemini 59%

Capricorn - Cancer 73%

Capricorn - Leo 69%

Capricorn – Virgo 71%

Capricorn - Libra 60%

Capricorn - Scorpio 66%

Capricorn - Sagittarius 63%

Capricorn – Capricorn 81%

Capricorn - Aquarius 68%

Capricorn - Pisces 65

CAPRICORN TAROT

The Precaution:

Capricorn is cautious; they have often been deceived in love, so now they do everything "calmly and please." It's like poker players: you rarely know what they have in hand. Have you ever tried Strip Poker? Give it a try.

The Ritual:

Capricorn likes rituals, meaning: courtship, foreplay, the central part, and the end of the relationship. The morning after, some of them even bring breakfast to bed, at least in the early days. Perhaps it's a bit of a routine, but once it's set in motion, it eventually goes into overdrive.

The Virtual:

Capricorn, in addition to the real world, has their virtual world. They are inclined toward the Internet and consider sex a game, and, as in the game, there are times and rules. However, they wait, because "only when the going gets tough, the tough get going," and Capricorn is tough.

The Hidden Side:

Even though they may not realize it, Capricorn has a somewhat masochistic side in their unconscious, and they kind of like it. They let their partner take the initiative because, no matter how it goes, "it will be a success anyway."

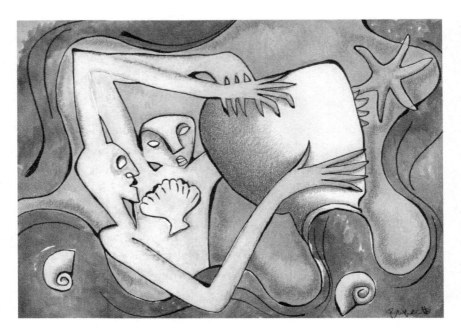

Aquarius - Air Sign –

Characteristics

You are characterized by stability. An idealist, everything revolves around your world. You are constant and firm in your decisions. You are proud to the point of megalomania, just to avoid giving in. You have a spirit of contradiction, you are the contrarian of the group. When you are angry, it's better to leave you alone; trying to change your mind would be pointless. You, Aquarius, always stand out for your originality and imagination. Kind-hearted and sometimes overly sincere. Sometimes, it's better not to give your opinion, especially if it's not requested. You have a strong spirit of independence, but you are committed to your family. You have a challenging character, but capable of extraordinary bursts of love. In a romantic relationship, you may appear tough to others, but you're tender in private.

General Horoscope 2024

A Year to Find Solutions

In 2024, Aquarius will face challenges and obstacles that will make you stronger. Even though success may not come quickly, and you may have to handle some financial difficulties, remember that every trial you face will make you more resilient.

Planetary Blessings:

With Jupiter's blessings in the second quarter and Venus's positive influence in the first half of the year, Aquarians will experience moments of happiness and contentment. These planets will favor various aspects of your life.

Struggle and Preparation:

Prepare to face significant challenges, especially with Pluto in the third quarter of 2024. Even though there will be difficulties, keep in mind that you have the strength to overcome them, and Jupiter will be there to help you navigate the chaos.

Personal Growth:

Uranus will demand your attention in your personal life, but thanks to Mars's positive influence, you will have the opportunity to improve many things. Personal growth will be a significant part of your year, so be ready to face new challenges.

Love and Marital Relationships:

The year promises love, especially in marital bonds. The Sun and Mars will bring blessings to your romantic relationships. However, those seeking a suitable partner might face some delays due to Saturn's delaying influence.

Transformation and Growth:

The stars suggest that 2024 will prepare you for transformation and growth in various aspects of your life, including professional, financial, and personal areas.

2024 will be a year of challenges and growth for Aquarius. Face difficulties with determination, leverage planetary blessings, and be prepared for significant personal growth. Your romantic relationships will thrive, although patience might be required in finding a suitable partner.

Aquarius - Love Horoscope 2024

In 2024, single Aquarians may experience delays in finding a suitable partner. The first half of the year might bring emotional ups and downs, but be patient, as the tables may turn in your favor soon.

Keeping Calm:

Relationships may be subjected to occasional disagreements and squabbles. It's essential to keep calm and maintain your mental health in these situations. Mutual understanding will be crucial to overcome challenges.

Reconciliation and Third Parties:

Some Aquarians might expect reconciliation with an ex-partner in the second half of the year. However, do your best to remain positive and handle these situations wisely. Some relationships might face interference from third parties, so it's important to take care of your partner to maintain a solid connection.

Challenges and Opportunities in Professional Life:

For some Aquarius couples, challenges related to professional matters may arise, affecting their relationship. However, starting new projects together could be an opportunity to strengthen the bond.

Balancing Work and Relationship:

The year will focus on balancing work and personal life. Maintain equilibrium between your professional responsibilities and the time you dedicate to your partner.

Resolution of Difficulties:

Married couples might face arguments and intense discussions, but it's essential to find peaceful solutions and mutual understanding. Legal proceedings might work in your favor in the second half of the year if you are seeking a legal resolution.

New Paths:

Those looking to start a new life together will find favorable opportunities in 2024. Don't dwell on past concerns; the future looks promising.

Upcoming Marriage:

Even individuals who postponed their wedding plans will find fortune towards the end of 2024, with the possibility of tying the knot or formalizing their engagement.

Romance and Love:

For married couples, the last quarter of the year promises romance, love, understanding, and empathy. Make the most of this time to strengthen your bond.

2024 will be a year of ups and downs in relationships for Aquarius. Stay calm, seek peaceful solutions, and leverage the opportunities that arise. Love and affection will be at the center of your life, so focus on nurturing your relationships.

Aquarius - Finance Horoscope 2024

To manage your finances in 2024, it's essential to maintain a positive mindset. Even though you may face challenges, keep confidence in your prudent ways and remain optimistic.

Strategic Investments:

The last quarter of the year will be a good time for financial investments. However, avoid impulsive trading and seek advice from experienced individuals. Prudent Management: Manage your finances strategically throughout the year. Clear and concise financial agreements will work in your favor.

Influx of Money:

In the middle of the year, you might experience a sudden influx of money, possibly related to legal matters or family properties. Use these funds wisely to advance your financial goals. Beneficial Collaborations: Collaborate with trusted individuals in your business, which could lead to significant financial progress. Travel-related businesses should also fare well.

Late Investments:

Significant financial investments will be more favorable in the second half of 2024, with planetary changes improving your financial situation. Gains from Personal Connections: Some Aquarians might benefit from personal connections in the financial sector. You'll also recover money lent to close individuals during this period.

Reinvestment and Savings:

Consider reinvesting old fixed deposits or other banked funds, as this could lead to gains. Purchasing property or assets like jewelry can be smart investments. Loan Issue Resolution: If you have loan problems, you'll see favorable results in the second quarter of 2024. You might even clear your debts.

Family Income and Stress:

Family income will be helpful, but budget management might be stressful at times. Keep expenses in check and plan carefully. Purchases and Legal Issues: Those planning to buy land or property might face legal issues in the first half of 2024. However, buying a vehicle could be a good option.

2024 calls for prudence and optimism in managing your finances. Seize tactical investment opportunities and stay focused on your financial goals. Personal connections could play a significant role in improving your financial situation. Pay attention to details and seek expert advice when needed to maximize your financial gains.

Aquarius - Career Horoscope 2024

In 2024, you may still face some challenges in your professional life. Your determined nature pushes you to avoid compromises, but you will find ways to overcome the obstacles you encounter.

If you work in the private sector, you might go through a period of intense work without immediate results. Your commitment and hard work will begin to improve your reputation around the third quarter.

Job Changes or Promotions:

If you're looking for a job change or a promotion, 2024 looks promising. Prepare with creative solutions to overcome any obstacles you may encounter along the way. Successful Business Ventures: You might consider starting a new venture with good chances of success, especially in collaboration with others. Travel-related businesses should perform well too.

Education and Learning:

Aquarius students might face some challenges in the first half of the year, but with dedication and perseverance, you'll achieve positive results. Additionally, your plans for further studies will take shape towards the end of the year.

Entry into the Professional World:

If you're aiming to enter the professional world, be prepared to overcome tests along the way. Work on improving your personality and skills, and gain confidence before proposing ideas in your work environment.

2024 will bring career challenges, but your determination and dedication will help you overcome them. Be open to new entrepreneurial opportunities and strive to continually enhance your skills. Maintain confidence in yourself and be prepared to find creative solutions to the obstacles that come your way.

Aquarius - Family Horoscope 2024

In 2024, family attention will remain important. Even though you might not consider it your primary duty, you will need to focus on managing the household and caring for your family. This will be a year where you have to take your share of family responsibilities.

Your younger siblings will continue to make significant progress in their professional lives. Meanwhile, older siblings might share news about their personal lives, possibly announcing new developments or additions to the family. These events will bring joy and happiness to your family.

Your parents will be engaged in social gatherings and might make new friends that will be beneficial for the family business. These interactions will also have a positive impact on your financial situation. However, you might find yourself in disagreement with your father on some issues due to differences between traditional and modern ideologies. Try to resolve these differences through open communication and mutual understanding.

You might encounter occasional difficulties in managing family finances, but your mother will be of great help in resolving these issues. Tensions regarding property might arise, but prospects for resolving these matters will be positive towards the end of the year. If you have plans to start something new, your family and friends will be willing to support you, but you'll need to demonstrate great confidence and conviction.

Annoying Relatives: In the third quarter of 2024, you might have to deal with some annoying relatives, but it's important to act wisely to avoid exacerbating family issues. Children in the Family: Children in the family will bring good news, including exceptional achievements, recognitions, and significant steps in their personal and professional growth. These events will contribute to the overall happiness of your family and strengthen emotional bonds among all of you.

In general, 2024 will be a year where family will be at the center of your life, and you will need to take care of your family responsibilities. It will also be a year of progress and joys for your family members, and any tensions can be overcome through communication and mutual understanding.

Aquarius - Health Horoscope 2024

In 2024, your health should remain a top priority. You should understand that good health is fundamental for a sound mind and for avoiding future issues. Even though you might face some challenges, it's crucial to take care of yourself promptly.

First Half of the Year: The first half of 2024 might present some health challenges. You might have to deal with seasonal illnesses or revisit old injuries. The key to overcoming these challenges is to seek appropriate treatment without delay. Listen carefully to medical advice and stay focused on your health.

Ongoing Treatments: If you're already undergoing medical treatment, you'll see positive progress, even if you don't initially achieve the desired results. Perseverance and optimism will be crucial for the success of your treatment. Meditation, yoga, and breathing exercises can further improve your mental and physical health.

Elderly Aquarians should pay particular attention to joint health and the digestive system due to planetary changes. If you have known allergies, avoid allergens, especially in the second half of 2024, when they might manifest more intensely.

Stress Management: If you're too busy with your professional life, try to avoid overwork, as it can lead to headaches, stress, and anxiety. Practice stress management methods like regular physical exercise, meditation, and open communication about your concerns with close people.

Pregnant Women: Pregnant women should pay special attention to their health and the well-being of the child. Maintain a balanced diet, follow a regular sleep schedule, and be cautious not to put yourself in dangerous situations. Be particularly careful during the middle months of 2024, as there might be an increased likelihood of accidents.

Exercise and Diet: Excessive physical exercise could lead to problems like sprains and strains. Focus on a balanced diet and control your workout routine to avoid injuries.

2024 requires constant attention to your health and well-being. Follow medical advice, adopt stress management practices, and maintain a balanced lifestyle to ensure that your health remains in good condition.

Couple Affinity

Him Aquarius

Aquarius - Aries 84%

Aquarius - Taurus 90%

Aquarius - Gemini 79%

Aquarius - Leo 77%

Aquarius - Virgo 76%

Aquarius - Libra 79%

Aquarius - Scorpio 67%

Aquarius - Sagittarius 83%

Aquarius - Capricorn 68%

Aquarius - Aquarius 75%

Aquarius - Pisces 58%

Couple Affinity

Her Aquarius

Aquarius - Aries 73%

Aquarius - Taurus 53%

Aquarius - Gemini 70%

Aquarius - Cancer 68%

Aquarius - Leo 81%

Aquarius - Virgo 78%

Aquarius - Libra 63%

Aquarius - Scorpio 59%

Aquarius - Sagittarius 84%

Aquarius - Capricorn 68%

Aquarius - Aquarius 75%

Aquarius - Pisces 68%

AQUARIUS TAROT

The Spanish

Aquarius has a strong and decisive character. They take matters seriously and provide security. They are not only jealous but possessive. What is theirs... is theirs! In their universe, the partner doesn't merge with them but becomes incorporated; if left alone, however, they despair, and the world collapses on them.

The Tongue

Aquarius, with some exceptions, is selfish in bed. Sometimes they even demand and have a preference for oral intercourse. The Tongue, for Aquarius, represents something more than just a muscle. So, at times, they might indulge in honey, cream, chocolate, and more.

The Traveler:

Aquarius, especially the man, is knowledgeable and usually well-endowed. They enjoy traveling, especially within people. When it comes to the sexual aspect, they have a lot of experience to offer. Also because there would be someone willing to buy it.

The Hidden Side:

The hidden side of Aquarius women is a predisposition for same-sex relationships. It might happen tomorrow, or it might never happen, but the predisposition is there, just like the one fo female friends. As for Aquarius men, their hidden desire could be a night with two women.

PISCE - Water Sign –

CHARACTERISTICS

You are characterized by Universal Love. Altruistic, sentimental, and romantic, you dream of peace in the world. You are more inclined towards the spirit than the body. Yoga, meditation, and homeopathy are your faith. You love tranquility, fantasy, and seek to understand others. You are emotional and easily impressionable. In a couple's relationship, you tend to be the weaker link, but you are not afraid of being alone. Despite everything, you, Pisces, dislike monotony. You are the quiet water that breaks bridges. You are willing to be a lover, but not forever. You always manage to attract the most beautiful, but at the same time, you sometimes lose them due to your innate emotional instability. There is no motto more fitting for Pisces than: "Liberty, Equality, Fraternity."

GENERAL HOROSCOPE 2024

A year to overcome challenges

2024 will be a year of changes and challenges for Pisces. You will be called upon to show your true potential and navigate through diverse situations with determination and wisdom. Planetary influences will put you to the test, but you will have the opportunity to grow and prosper.

Career:

In 2024, your career will require more attention and planning. You will need to reflect on where you want your professional life to take you and plan accordingly. Although you may face moments of slowdown, the planet Mars will be an important ally in helping you overcome obstacles. Be patient and determined, and you will see progress in your career.

Finances:

From a financial perspective, 2024 will bring favorable results for Pisces. You will enjoy a greater influx of money compared to previous years, and you will feel a sense of prosperity. However, be aware of moments when Saturn slows things down. Maintain prudent financial management and plan your investments wisely.

Health:

In the second half of 2024, your focus will shift to health. Thanks to the positive influence of Jupiter, your well-being will improve, and persistent health issues may get better. Dedicate time to self-care and follow a balanced diet and a healthy lifestyle to maximize your well-being.

Love and Relationships:

In 2024, you may feel distant from relationships due to the influence of Pluto. There may be challenges in your love life, but Venus and Mercury will be your allies in overcoming them. Be open to communication and mutual understanding. Relationships will require commitment and work, but they can lead to greater stability and happiness.

Other Challenges:

The influences of Uranus could bring challenges in other areas of your life. However, as always, you will be a fighter and face challenges with courage and determination. Seize the opportunities that arise and continue to show your resilient spirit.

2024 will require Pisces to reflect, plan, and commit. It will be a year of personal and professional growth, and the challenges you face will help you become a stronger and more aware person. Maintain a positive mindset and approach the year with confidence.

Pisces - Love Horoscope 2024

024 begins on a positive note for Pisces in love. Couples will be full of love and spend precious time together. Even with busy schedules, the planetary transits of the year will work in your favor to create stronger connections with your partner. The first quarter of the year is a good time to plan romantic getaways and address any recent relationship issues. For those who have just started dating, there may be some initial moments of uncertainty, but don't be discouraged, as things will improve over time.

Marriage and Commitment:

If you are looking to find a partner to marry, 2024 may bring good news. The middle months of the year will be favorable for those seeking a serious commitment. However, it is important to proceed with caution, as there may be some challenges and disagreements along the way. Be patient and communicate openly to overcome any obstacles.

Existing Relationships:

For those already in a committed relationship, the first half of the year will be a favorable time to embark on new adventures with your partner. Avoid investing too much money in shared projects, as there may be a risk of financial losses. Communication and mutual understanding will be crucial to the success of your relationship.

Difficulties and Challenges:

The influences of Uranus could bring some challenges in other areas of your life, and there may be difficult and emotional moments. However, remember that you are a fighter and can face any challenge with courage and determination.

Your friendships will play an important role in your love life, and you may meet someone special through a close friend or acquaintance.

Complex Situations:

For those in complex situations such as breakups, divorces, or toxic relationships, 2024 could bring relief. Legal matters will work in your favor, and you will have the opportunity to start a new life. It may take time to heal from past traumas, but by the end of the year, you will find someone better to build a healthier and more lasting relationship with.

2024 will be a year of ups and downs in love for Pisces, but with commitment, patience, and open communication, you can overcome any challenge and build stronger and more meaningful relationships. Be open to love and the possibility of new connections, and remain confident in your love journey.

Pisces - Finance Horoscope 2024

2024 will be a year when Pisces should pay special attention to their finances. While the pressure to earn may not be your primary concern, it is essential to have a guide for responsible financial management. Fortunately, there are no signs of significant financial problems in your horoscope, and the planet Mars will help you understand how money can be a long-term ally.

Saving and Investments:

During the second quarter of the year, thanks to Jupiter's influence, you will enjoy good financial gains. It will be a favorable time to explore new investment opportunities. You may encounter people who introduce you to the concept of long-term savings and investment, which will help you build a solid financial foundation.

Legal Issues and Property:

However, Saturn could create some complications for those dealing with legal matters related to property. Nevertheless, towards the end of the fourth quarter, there may be good news in this area. Purchasing property, especially in the last quarter, will be a favorable move for you. If you are interested in buying jewelry, the second quarter of 2024 will be the ideal time to do so.

Expenses and Business Investments:

Be cautious with expenses and try not to overspend, as this could lead to financial problems. Your career choices will be crucial to your overall financial situation, so make wise decisions in this area. Entrepreneurs will need to expand their businesses to accumulate wealth, and the last quarter of the year will see a significant increase in earnings for those doing business abroad.

Consultation and New Investments:

If you are considering new investments or starting a new venture, avoid rushing until the last quarter of 2024. Take the time to plan carefully and seek advice from experts who can guide you in your financial decisions.

2024 offers positive financial opportunities for Pisces, but it is essential to manage finances carefully, avoid excessive spending, and invest wisely. With careful planning and a responsible approach, you can enjoy a prosperous and stable financial year.

Pisces - Career Horoscope 2024

2024 will be a year of changes and challenges in your career, dear Pisces. If you are contemplating a major career change, it is essential to proceed with caution. For at least the first half of the year, the planets suggest taking a step back and carefully reflecting on your professional choices. Rushing is not an option at this time. Before embarking on a new path, make sure you fully understand the implications and your current needs. If you feel that something is missing in your current career, make an effort to identify and address these gaps rather than seeking easy solutions.

Success and Results:

Around the middle of the year, your career may take a backseat for some of your colleagues, as you may enjoy success and positive results. However, do not let this success distract you from your professional responsibilities. There may be opportunities for mistakes or unintended consequences if you are not vigilant. If you are involved in business partnerships or have international connections, be prepared for challenges such as investments or delays in negotiations.

Students and Education:

Pisces students will have a favorable year in 2024. You will be able to pass most of your exams and achieve excellent academic performance by the end of the year. Preparations for higher education and pursuing your dream college will go as planned. However, avoid distractions and stay focused on your goals. Listen to the advice of your supporters, as they may offer valuable guidance on the path to follow. If you are preparing for competitive exams, 2024 will be favorable for you. Make the most of your study time and prepare diligently, especially if you have exams in the first half of the year.

Promotions and Professional Development:

For those who have worked hard in previous years, there will be opportunities for promotions and career advancements. In the second half of 2024, with the right strategy and effective communication, you will achieve your professional goals. Travel will be advantageous for your professional development, so connect with the right people during your travels. Additionally, your superiors will recognize projects you have handled excellently. For those starting their careers, the second half of the year will bring job opportunities. Although there may be obstacles and delays, investing in your skills will help you find the right job or your dream job.

2024 will require patience and attention in your career. If you face challenges with determination and commitment, you will have the opportunity to achieve success and realize your professional goals throughout the year.

Pisces - Family Horoscope 2024

2024 will require effort and patience from you to maintain family harmony, dear Pisces. Younger family members may be challenging to handle, with possible arguments and issues. If you have siblings, be prepared for disagreements about how to manage the family business, with some wanting a different direction than you had in mind. However, do not let these disagreements create permanent divisions; instead, seek dialogue and compromise solutions.

Professional Success:

In the second half of 2024, some family members may receive good news in their careers. There may be new jobs, promotions, or improvements in their current careers, which will have a positive impact on family finances. If your family has faced financial issues, such as loans or debts, be prepared to receive good news as these issues begin to resolve.

Family Health:

Elderly family members may expect an improvement in their health, although they may not be completely out of the woods. Nevertheless, you will see significant progress in their treatments and relief from long-standing concerns.

New Life in the Family:

Pisces couples can expect the arrival of a new life in their family. Expectant mothers should pay special attention to their health, as there may be some challenges in the third quarter. Children may give you a hard time with their mood swings, but these moments will be temporary. Be prepared to take care of household chores in the third quarter, as it will be a time to settle things at home.

Family Challenges:

Towards the end of the year, you may face some family challenges. There may be disagreements with your father regarding financial decisions, while your mother may have health issues. However, these difficulties will not last long, and by the last quarter of the year, the situation will stabilize. Despite potential obstacles and disagreements, keep in mind that many of these situations will be resolved in the first half of the year. Continue to seek dialogue and maintain an open mind to preserve family harmony.

2024 will require patience, understanding, and dialogue in your family. Approach challenges with maturity and try to resolve them constructively. With commitment and love, you will be able to maintain a harmonious family environment despite the difficulties that may arise along the way.

Pisces - Health Horoscope 2024

2024 will bring good news for your health, dear Pisces. The first half of the year will be a period of well-being, with the treatments you have undergone finally showing positive results. You will be satisfied with your health conditions, allowing you to relax and enjoy life. However, for those who have spent a lot of time on physical training, there may be a feeling of exhaustion. It is important to listen to your body and adjust your training according to your needs and energy levels.

Fitness Goals:

If you have set fitness goals for the new year, 2024 offers good opportunities to achieve them. Although there may be distractions along the way, your commitment and determination will be crucial to maintaining your health goals. Try to overcome any obstacles that may arise and keep your motivation high.

Diet:

Pay attention to your diet in the second half of the year. If you have had poor eating habits, consider making improvements to your diet. Avoid unhealthy foods and excessive drinks, especially around the middle of the year. Maintain a balanced diet and try to introduce healthier foods into your daily routine.

Children's Eye Health:

For Pisces children, 2024 could bring eye problems if they spend too much time in front of electronic devices. Encourage them to reduce screen time and engage in outdoor physical activities. This will not only improve their concentration but also protect their visual health.

Need for Rest:

In the second half of the year, you may feel the need for a break and a period of rest to recharge your energy. This is especially true for professionals who may be under work-related stress. Take time for yourself and try to relieve stress through relaxing activities.

Seasonal Changes:

Around the third quarter, there may be some flu-like conditions due to changes in planetary positions. Take care of yourself, avoid outside food, and be prepared for these seasonal changes.

2024 offers good opportunities to improve your health and well-being. Listen to your body, maintain a balanced lifestyle, and tackle any health challenges with determination. With care and awareness, you will be able to face any health challenges that may arise during the year.

Couple Affinity

Him Pisces

Pisces - Aries 59%

Pisces - Taurus 84%

Pisces - Gemini 76%

Pisces - Cancer 71%

Pisces - Leo 58%

Pisces - Virgo 85%

Pisces - Libra 75%

Pisces - Scorpio 89%

Pisces - Sagittarius 78%

Pisces - Capricorn 75%

Pisces - Aquarius 68%

Pisces - Pisces 69%

Couple Affinity

Her Pisces

Pisces - Aries 56%

Pisces - Taurus 82%

Pisces - Gemini 57%

Pisces - Cancer 89%

Pisces - Leo 75%

Pisces - Virgo 69%

Pisces - Libra 69%

Pisces - Scorpio 61%

Pisces - Sagittarius 71%

Pisces - Capricorn 69%

Pisces - Aquarius 58%

Pisces - Pisces 69%

Pisces Tarot

The Orgasm:

Both male and female Pisces are altruistic; they prioritize their partner's pleasure over their own. Pisces, in terms of eroticism, always knows what to do and, more importantly, how to do it. The partner with them always remains satisfied, at least in the sexual sphere.

The Witch:

The female Pisces is a Witch, both in how she manages to bewitch her partner and because she is very attracted to the occult. However, Pisces individuals, too, are true Magicians; they can enchant with just their words. We can say that being with Pisces is definitely a magical experience.

The Moody One:

Pisces is a dual sign, with two personalities. "Moody" is certainly an appropriate term: if they don't like someone, Pisces might, after a fantastic aperitif and dinner, arrive at the doorstep and, at the most beautiful moment, bid farewell with two kisses on the cheek and a "Goodbye and thank you."

The Hidden Side:

The not-so-hidden side of Pisces is that they need an Elastic Relationship. For them, an occasional sexual adventure is sometimes part of the game. They need their freedom. If caught, they would come out with a candid "It was just sex; with you, I make love."

Couple Affinity

LGBTQIA+

Him - Him / Her - Her

	♈	♈	♉	♊	♋	♌	♍	♎	♏	♐	♑	♒	♓	
♈	89	90	73	68	65	61	59	78	73	78	63	87	69	♈
♉	75	71	75	71	87	83	76	87	92	83	69	93	88	♉
♊	69	63	88	88	81	69	65	90	91	86	78	84	79	♊
♋	61	74	65	71	72	68	81	79	82	82	73	70	74	♋
♌	73	62	75	73	63	64	59	94	81	85	83	79	63	♌
♍	62	78	85	66	83	84	86	74	76	63	81	78	87	♍
♎	88	89	74	73	91	73	80	79	71	74	85	84	79	♎
♏	89	83	83	83	62	79	83	92	92	60	79	69	91	♏
♐	83	87	81	86	78	69	79	69	77	78	79	87	80	♐
♑	71	79	69	76	76	74	69	71	68	84	85	74	69	♑
♒	76	61	79	63	84	81	69	63	88	75	79	78	74	♒
♓	66	87	63	91	77	74	74	69	75	73	69	74	73	♓
	♈	♉	♊	♋	♌	♍	♎	♏	♐	♑	♒	♓	♓	

Horoscope 2024 - LGBT QIA+

ARIES

- Fire Sign -

Astrology in 2024 maps possibilities and relationships for all LGBT AI+ individuals as they unfold over time, respecting the mystery of how things develop. Just as meteorologists can't always predict a storm, you too should allow yourself to be curious but not cling too tightly to a particular version of the future, especially in a time when everything is still quite hazy and largely uncertain.

2024 will be the year when your life changes, as well as the world around you, concerning your desire for freedom and collective responsibility. The climate of affection and relationships will change dramatically. Mid-year, you'll need a break to see this new world a bit more clearly, even if you can't define it yet. In the bigger picture, you are still in a period of total changes, which probably won't stabilize until all the outer planets finish their transit through a new sign in 2025.

So, be particularly gentle with yourself, and in 2024, take all the time you need to consider, contemplate, and desire the type of love you want.

TAURUS

- Earth Sign -

Rest is the real theme this year. From this perspective, 2024 is a year to catch your breath and relax as you prepare for another "Tour de Force." 2024 might bring some confusion as you transition from years of constant pressure to a year of complete relaxation. Who wouldn't want a break?

anuary will be a slow and mostly sweet month. It's best to spend it ignoring those ads encouraging you to join a gym or pursue your potential project immediately. Instead, let your potential rest a bit, pamper yourself with a truly interesting book you've wanted to read, learn to cook something delicious, call distant friends. Don't rush to get anywhere concrete for now. Take the time you need to adjust to the changes, even if they are changes you desired or initiated yourself.

Rest, even when it seems like you should stay up all night worrying. There's a network of love and affection ready to support you. Even Mercury contributes to the slowness of this period. Let 2024 flow at its own pace, and love will be there when you are ready.

GEMINI

Air Sign -

2024 is the year when your happiness becomes contagious. It will restore your curiosity and sense of humor, allowing you to aim high once again, even if you approach your goal slowly. Despite the long and winding path you're on, you won't have to suddenly veer in another direction.

The tricky thing about 2024 is that it offers hope more than certainty. With Jupiter in Pisces, we tend to believe in what we want to believe. We want to believe that things will go well. We want to believe that love can conquer all, in a reality where everything can be magical. In the best of all possible worlds, this transition will help us believe that another world is possible, increasing our capacity for social cohesion through empathy and understanding sensitivity as strength.

Remember that you can love someone and still have healthy boundaries for how you want them to be in your life. Saying no to a toxic type of relationship makes it easier to create space for the relationships you desire.

CANCER

- *Water Sign* -

The past two years have been dominated by conflicts between the dark power of seeking intense emotions and the affairs in the power game. Rewriting the rules of your life will be essential if you truly want to change.

You'll need to emerge from your cocoon if you genuinely want to become a butterfly. You've had enough time to relax on a leaf, letting your wings dry in the sun. Now is the time to fly. You must use your abilities to broaden your horizons, change your perspective on the here and now, learn to respect people and, above all, your deadlines.

You need to become a part of a bigger world, reach the next level, and remove your safety net to avoid feeling trapped by always playing the same game.

Expand your desire to explore; don't settle for the first choice. Learn to trust your instincts, and 2024 will reward you by helping you understand when and how to move towards what you desire, and even better, towards what you love.

LEO

- Fire Sign -

Whether you were single or in a relationship, with or without friends, it was challenging to shake off a deep sense of loneliness last year. In 2024, it doesn't have to be that way anymore.

Start considering that loneliness is a feeling you need to seriously address, even admitting your own shortcomings. Learn to differentiate between what can become something serious and what only brings you temporary joy.

Learn to choose the kind of person who loves you for who you are, in your entirety, not just when you shine and impress, but also when you're sometimes selfish, ordinary, or boring.

It's a love that could work with you to prioritize what you can build together, commit to the project of growing together. Are you ready to grow and commit to being loved in this way and to offer this kind of love? Are you ready to leave loneliness behind and build something special with the person you love?

VIRGO

- Earth Sign -

2024 will be the year in which you revolutionize your life. But I don't want you to think of it in literal terms, like something violent or taken for granted. I want you to think about what you see happening every day in your life, and every time you see it, say, "This needs to change." Well, the time has come to do it.

Think about how your world, your life, could be different, just by making small changes without revolutionizing it. Consider what small actions you could take regularly to support this change. Start taking the first steps, or rather, take the first step towards things that provide relief.

The map of 2024 should be a map of actions aimed at improving your life, your work, your health, but above all, your relationships and love. You've reached a point where you need to question yourself, where you need to refine your qualities and abilities. Start demanding from yourself what you also demand from others, but, more importantly, what you can offer to yourself that will benefit others. In 2024, ask yourself this question and provide an answer.

LIBRA

- Air Sign -

Do you want to know what beautiful change 2024 will bring you? Well, dear Libra, many of the pressures of 2023 are easing for you, and the new energy from the influence of other planets is stimulating your innate need for creativity, playfulness, and romance.

If your current relationship situation doesn't satisfy you, don't worry, especially if it leans too much towards your partner's or others' needs and interests. 2024 will be the year when you start balancing it with your own needs, regardless of whether your friends or lovers share this choice.

This year, you'll learn more about your nature, and we're not just talking about sexual desire but also what makes life joyful and fulfilling. It's time to chart some new paths. Focus your energies on something productive or worthy of your time.

Repaint the canvas of your life, rewrite your story, dress with care, take selfies, and change your profile picture. You'll find that flirting, romance, and exciting new friendships won't be in short supply for you in 2024.

SCORPIO

- *Water Sign* -

You carry wounds from the past inflicted by others that haven't healed yet. Scorpio, 2024 won't be easy for you unless you can internalize the past and leap into the future.

An incredible year of opportunities awaits you, but only if you can seize them. You have the wisdom of the past guiding you, which can make you suspicious of others, but in 2024, you must give people who want to work with you to positively change your "Status Quo" a chance.

This means drawing deeply from your roots but orienting yourself toward an unknown future, always treating your pain with love and attention but not allowing it to dictate your future. Create a family in the broadest sense with those you trust and mutually respect.

2024 will be a year of intense changes for you, and you may not always welcome them, but you can always count on those who love you and have been with you even in difficult times.

SAGITTARIUS

- Fire Sign -

How well you design and plan this magnificent 2024 will determine your future. So, what this year asks of you is not to rely on your flexible, adaptable, and adventurous side but rather to notice what you've overlooked when diving into a new adventure.

There are issues you can solve on your own, but in some cases in 2024, you'll need to learn to ask for help. There are conversations you need to face but have avoided. You'll need the courage to confront reality, even if there are moments of eclipse. Only then will 2024 be your magical year.

This year, everything you've tried to ignore will come to the surface and demand your attention. Start now, with small steps, to resolve your persistent issues. Remember that you can use your words and not just your imagination. Be specific about what you want to achieve this year. Listen more closely to what the people you care about are saying. Allow yourself to be surprised and loved.

CAPRICORN

- Earth Sign -

2024 is the year when you must change paradigms, shift from negativity, and embrace the idea that things can and will go well. I know it hasn't always been the case in recent years, but try to imagine a 2024 filled with money, love, support, learning experiences, sex, food, and more.

Take at least one moment to trust that taking a risk or taking a break won't put you in a difficult situation. Believe in yourself and fight for your creative ideas with the people you enjoy sharing them with.

When things get tough, you have your evacuation backpack ready. In intimacy, remember that you have a lot to give and don't always remember that you have the right to receive. Because in love, it's not always the one who runs away that wins, in fact, almost never.

These should be your goals for 2024: increase your capacity by increasing your resources so you can be prepared for all the surprises that come your way.

AQUARIUS

- Air Sign -

2024 - The Show Must Go On - The show must go on. It's time to look beyond; you can't stop, and you shouldn't return to your old life now that the pandemic is over.

If you need to finish school or a course, if you need to look for another job because your current one doesn't satisfy you, if you need to cut ties with your ex who complicates your life with the person you now love, do it. Do it now! Do it in 2024; don't wait!

There are experiences you've had in recent years that have prepared you for the next phase of your life. Don't fear reverting to who you were before. You're a different person now, a new person. Love yourself for who you are and as you are.

Any opportunity you can take or miss this year, the choices must always be yours, without being influenced by anyone. Remember that love, whatever it may be, triumphs over everything.

PISCES

- Water Sign -

"Ama il Tuo Sogno, Se pur ti tormenta," said an Italian poet. 2024 is the right year to reclaim your dream. It's normal that as we age, we start giving up on certain dreams. Not everyone will become an astronaut, a footballer, a famous singer, or a prima ballerina. But what happens to the parts of you that are still tied to these dreams?

For many Pisces, who, as we know, are peculiar due to the dominance of Uranus in the sign, 2023 was a year of deferred dreams or perhaps dreams completely cut off from their lives. Maybe you've learned to dream purely as fantasy or compulsively watching your reflection in a well-produced TV show where you dreamed of being the protagonist.

I'm not saying that 2024 will be the year when you realize everything you've ever dreamed of, but it's worth revisiting some dreams you gave up on, perhaps a little too soon, and that may still be achievable. If you have even the slightest chance, seize it. In love, "...do it differently..."

Printed in Great Britain
by Amazon

39251001R00096